# ON THE ROAD

# ON THE ROAD

COMPILED BY WILLIAM MARSHALL DUKE AND RICK SCHATZ

**MEDITATIONS FOR
MEN WHO TRAVEL**

BEACON HILL PRESS
OF KANSAS CITY

# FOREWORD

Over 59,000 hotels, motels, and bed-and-breakfast inns dot the landscape along the major roadways and thoroughfares of these United States.[1] On weekday evenings, many of the occupants of these venues are individuals who are "on the road" for business-related reasons. The United States Department of Transportation recently reported that over 405 million long-distance trips (that is, trips of over 50 miles from home) were for business purposes, accounting for 16 percent of all long-distance trips in the country. Records indicate that 77 percent, or 8 of every 10 of those trips, were taken by men.[2]

Hotel ownership recognizes the lucrative advantage of housing business representatives and goes to extremes to cater to those customers. Spacious rooms—some nearly 800 square feet—combine both work space and bedroom accommodations. The business traveler doesn't tend to work a defined set of hours, so hotels provide not just a table and a chair but also a "workstation," where a guest can pursue business assignments while sitting in a "desk chair" illuminated with office-style lighting. Internet connectivity—often wireless—is a standard feature. Many hotels offer fax services and have printers and photocopiers in a "business center" as well.

Indoor swimming pools and exercise rooms are common, some of which have phones positioned by the equipment so an individual can both exercise and converse with clients (if not using his or her own cell phone). Lounges, sports bars, and snack centers are frequently provided in hotels catering to the business traveler, where one can eat, relax, and unwind. In an effort to help the business traveler, some hotels offer a "happy-hour" or "guest receptions" in late afternoons, in which a dinner of sorts can be enjoyed. Many even pack a "breakfast bag" for the traveler who has to dash off to an airport for an early-morning flight.

It seems every detail is addressed relating to the business traveler, including in-room options for television viewing. While one may not find as many channels as are available at home, the business traveler is almost assured access to the "essential" channels. He or she can keep track of the latest developments on Wall Street over business-oriented networks. One can also expect that there will be CNN and/or FOX News as well as NBC, CBS, and ABC outlets. The Weather Channel and multiple sports channels are included in the package. Typically one or more of the so-called "premium channels," such as HBO and Cinemax, are offered as well. Statistics shared by a national media company indicate that 98 percent of hotel guests turn on the television set when they enter the room.[3] Hotels situate the television set to be the focal point of the room, and guests watch an average of 4.5 hours per day.[4] All these viewing opportunities are included *free* as a part of the room rental.

But many hotels go a step further and offer pay-per-view programming.[5] For a fee, an individual can choose to view a range of recent movie releases, many labeled "R" or "Adult Programming." Lodgenet, the leading purveyor of pay-per-view in North America, reported recently that it is available in more than 1.9 million rooms in 10,000 properties worldwide and reaching more than 500 million travelers annually.[6] Many of these pay-per-view selections would not be chosen by the family who's traveling on vacation, but companies hope to capitalize on the fact that an individual in the room *alone* may choose to invest both time and money in their products. According to *Promo Magazine,* "Hotels offer a unique environment for companies to find a captive audience"[7] that is in an "experimental and exploratory mode."[8]

Since 77 percent of business travelers are men, the appeal to man's visually-stimulated side for entertainment can often be drawn to one of the premium channels, to the pay-per-view options, or to computer web sites. The man on the road is by himself, is perhaps lonely, is tired from a busy day and evening, and is in an isolated, private environment where nobody is the wiser. The businessman on the road is just one click away from programming that can prove to be detrimental to him, to his marriage, to his children, to his finances, and to his whole lifestyle.

Peter and Paul, two stalwarts in the faith, specifically addressed the fact that Satan is always seeking an entry point into one's life and that he is carefully looking for weak areas he can exploit. Peter pleads, "Keep a cool head. Stay alert. The Devil is poised to pounce, and would like nothing better than to catch you napping" (1 Peter 5:8, TM). Paul warns,

> God is strong, and he wants you strong. So take everything the Master has set out for you, well-made weapons of the best materials. And put them to use so you will be able to stand up to everything the Devil throws your way. This is no afternoon athletic contest that we'll walk away from and forget about in a couple of hours. This is for keeps, a life-or-death fight to the finish against the Devil and all his angels (*Ephesians 6:10-12*, TM).

Paul continues with wise counsel in his letters. In Galatians 5:16-21 he admonishes us to—

> Live by the Spirit and you will not gratify the desires of the sinful nature. For the sinful nature desires what is contrary to the Spirit, and the Spirit what is contrary to the sinful nature. They are in conflict with each other, so that you do not do what you want. But if you are led by the Spirit, you are not under law. The acts of the sinful nature are obvious: sexual immorality, impurity and debauchery; idolatry and witchcraft; hatred, discord, jealousy, fits of rage, selfish ambition, dissensions, factions and envy;

drunkenness, orgies, and the like. I warn you, as I did before, that those who live like this will not inherit the kingdom of God.

"Get into their rooms and stay on their minds" is a business slogan adhered to by both advertisers and the creators of all sorts of "entertainment." In his concluding remarks to the Christians living in the Roman colony of Philippi, Paul addressed the importance of man filling his mind with productive thoughts:

> Summing it all up, friend, I'd say you'll do your best by filling your minds and meditating on things true, noble, reputable, authentic, compelling, gracious—the best, not the worst; the beautiful, not the ugly; things to praise, not things to curse. Put into practice what you learned from me; what you heard and saw and realized. Do that, and God, who makes everything work together, will work you into his most excellent harmonies (*Philippians 4:8-9, TM*).

*On the Road* is a collection of devotionals written by men for men. It is meant to be an alternative for the man who finds himself in a hotel and wants to do just as Paul recommended: "to fill [his] mind and meditate on beneficial things" rather than things that will bring harm to that which is most precious to him: his relationship with God, his family, and others. Fifty-four individuals from a wide range of vocational perspectives, cultures, races, and denominational affiliations contributed devotionals around eight themes: sexual purity, marriage, fathering, spiritual disciplines, prayer, godly characteristics, the centrality of Christ, and godly living.

It is our sincere hope and prayer that these devotionals will speak to men *On the Road* and give them strength, wisdom, and guidance as they seek to be men after God's own heart in their personal, professional, and spiritual lives.

---

*William Marshall Duke is the coordinator of men's ministries for the Church of the Nazarene. Rick Schatz is president & CEO of the National Coalition for the Protection of Children and Families.*

# MINISTERING TO PEOPLE "ON THE ROAD"

STEVE DOUGLASS ·····················································

*One of the wonderful benefits to being on the road is that we encounter new people, many of whom need the Lord or need the encouragement of a fellow believer.*

Jesus was on the road a lot, and many of His ministry opportunities arose in that context.

In John 4 we see Jesus traveling from Judea to Galilee through Samaria. As He rested by a well near Sychar, He encountered a Samarian woman. The end result was that she and many other Samaritans became believers.

On another occasion Jesus was passing through Jericho on His way to Jerusalem. Zacchaeus was the wealthy chief tax collector of Jericho who climbed up into a tree to be able to see Jesus as He passed by. To this man's surprise, Jesus stopped in front of the tree and said, "Zacchaeus, come down immediately. I must stay at your house today" (Luke 19:5). After spending some time with Jesus, Zacchaeus experienced a deep change of heart, which caused Jesus to observe, "Today salvation has come to this house, because this man, too, is a son of Abraham. For the Son of Man came to seek and to save what was lost" (Luke 19:9-10).

One of the benefits to being on the road is that we encounter people who need the Lord or the encouragement of another believer.

Some time ago I was flying from Frankfurt to Chicago. As I struck up a conversation with the woman sitting next to me, I discovered that her husband was in the Army in Iraq. He had been there for three months and was going to be there another year. She was distraught, to say the least, so I gave her a copy of my book *Enjoying Your Walk with God,* because the subtitle is *How to Live Above Your Everyday Circumstances.*

As the conversation continued, I sensed she was already a Christian but needed to know how to appropriate God's power and peace. So we walked through the part of the book that explains the Spirit-filled life. At the end she prayed and asked God to give her His peace through the power of His Spirit. She was crying, so she pulled out her compact and began to dry off her cheeks.

Then all of a sudden she turned to me and said, "I've been praying for you for the last week."

"Excuse me?" I said. "We just met."

She said, "I know, but a week ago I prayed that God would send someone to explain to me how to walk with Him."

God is amazing! He orchestrates circumstances so we can share what we know about Him so people can come to walk with Him.

Pray that God will prepare the hearts of strangers and bring them across your path as you are on the road.

---

*Steve Douglass is president of Campus Crusade for Christ.*

# A LIFE-CHANGING PRAYER

JERRY KIRK ······································································

In the mid 1960s two business leaders in Pittsburgh heard Sam Shoemaker's last sermon, "Get Changed, Get Together, and Get Going." Don Reyberg said to Kirwan Flannery, "We've been changed by Jesus Christ. Let's get together in order to get going."

They met the following Wednesday and asked for God's guidance to "get going." They invited men who were out of work to meet for lunch on Wednesdays with the promise that they would listen to each other's concerns, open themselves to each other and to Jesus Christ, and pray daily for work.

I saw the love of Christ in these two men and asked Don Reyberg to tell his story to a group of Christian leaders. While traveling to that meeting, I asked what God was doing in his life, and he told one story after another of men finding Christ and finding work. In 18 months nearly 350 men had come to the lunches, opened their lives to Christ, and found work. Employment Anonymous was born.

The more he talked, the more excited I became. "Don Reyberg, I don't know a preacher in America who could tell those life-changing stories, and you're the busiest layman I know."

Don said to me, "Do you want to be that kind of preacher?"

"I would give anything to be that kind of preacher."

"Do you want to enter into a 30-day prayer covenant?"

"Help me know what that means."

"Individually we pray at the beginning of every day for 30 days, *Jesus, be the Lord of my life today in new ways,* and we give as much of ourselves as we can to as much of Jesus as we understand. And when we do, we pray that same prayer for each other." Second Chronicles 15:12 says, "They entered into a covenant to seek the LORD, the God of their fathers, with all their heart and soul." That's what we do when we ask Jesus to be Lord.

This simple prayer changed my life and ministry in the summer of 1967. I don't know what I was doing before, but that prayer opened my life to the Spirit in new ways, and almost every person who came for counseling wanted to enter into a 30-day prayer covenant.

I've entered into hundreds of 30-day prayer covenants over the years. I'm in a number of such covenants today. But I've enlarged the specific prayer that I pray daily and to which I invite people. Change it, use it, and share it any way you choose. As you travel this month, consider making this your daily prayer each morning. It's a life-changing prayer that lasts a lifetime.

*Jesus, be the Lord of my life today in new ways. Live your life in me and through me. Change me any way you want. Wash me clean from every sin. Fill me with your Holy Spirit. I pray in Jesus' name. Amen.* ▐▊▐

---

*Jerry R. Kirk is the founder and chairman of the board of National Coalition for the Protection of Children & Families.*

# PORNOGRAPHY: OVERTURNING THE MONEY-CHANGERS' TABLES

PHILLIP COSBY ·····························································

*On reaching Jerusalem, Jesus entered the temple area and began driving out those who were buying and selling there. He overturned the tables of the money changers and the benches of those selling doves, and would not allow anyone to carry merchandise through the temple courts. And as he taught them, he said, "Is it not written: 'My house will be called a house of prayer for all nations'? But you have made it 'a den of robbers'" (Mark 11:15-17).*

As we look to Jesus as our example, we see a physically deliberate Jesus as He confronted the commercial prostitution of the Temple in Jerusalem. All four of the gospels record this dramatic and deliberate confrontation twice—first at the beginning of His ministry in John 2:11-17 and again just prior to His crucifixion in Matthew 21: 12-13; Mark 11: 15-17; and Luke 19:45-46.

Jesus was not just having a bad day! His act of making whips, driving all commercial interests from the Temple, overturning tables and chairs, and forbidding anyone from carrying wares through the

13

Temple is a violent scene that was planned, intentional, and forcefully executed. Why didn't Jesus just reason with the commercial interests? What's so special about the dwelling place of God's presence that evoked such zeal? What is the value of a strong physical statement? What does it mean for us today as we find courage to show up and confront a sexualized culture?

Recognize this? Sex sells! The sex business has profited immensely from the prostitution of the intended dwelling place of God's Holy Spirit. The compromising of a person's sexual integrity is unlike any other sin. Genuine compassionate Christianity cannot flow from a self-gratifying, polluted vessel no matter how generous.

Think this position is too extreme? Consider this passage, in 1 Corinthians 6:18-20—"Flee from sexual immorality. All other sins a man commits are outside his body, but he who sins sexually sins against his own body. Do you not know that your body is a temple of the Holy Spirit, who is in you, whom you have received from God? You are not your own; you were bought at a price. Therefore honor God with your body."

Technology has made highly sexualized and addictive images readily available. Nowhere are men more vulnerable than in a quiet hotel room, where they are alone and it seems that no one sees. But God sees. His voice is calling us to self-examination just as He does in Revelation 2 when walking among the seven churches identifying and calling His people to repentance from the sin of sexual immorality.

So you've failed—who hasn't? Getting off the sidelines and showing up is 90 percent of the battle. There is mercy and forgiveness in abundance, but "[make] the most of every opportunity, because the days are evil" (Ephesians 5:16).  ▥

---

*Phillip Cosby is the Executive Director of the Kansas City office of National Coalition for the Protection of Children and Families.*

# FINDING REST FOR A WEARY LIFE

DAVID GRAVES ⟩⟩⟩⟩⟩⟩⟩⟩⟩⟩⟩⟩⟩⟩⟩⟩⟩⟩⟩⟩⟩⟩⟩⟩⟩⟩⟩⟩⟩⟩⟩⟩⟩⟩⟩⟩⟩⟩⟩⟩⟩⟩⟩⟩⟩⟩⟩⟩

*Come to me, all you who are weary and burdened, and I will give you rest. Take my yoke upon you and learn from me, for I am gentle and humble in heart, and you will find rest for your souls. For my yoke is easy and my burden is light* (Matthew 11:28-30).

Michael Boyer wrote an article for the *National Geographic* titled "A Work-Weary World?" that may give us a little comfort. He notes that Americans are famous for their work ethic.

However, according to a study by the International Labor Organization, we're no longer the world leaders in hours worked per year. South Korea's booming economy necessitates a six-day work week. In the past few years, South Koreans have averaged 2,390 hours of work per year, as compared to the 1,792 hours of work per year in the United States. Workers in Japan, Poland, Australia, and New Zealand also worked more hours than U.S. workers. Swedish workers clocked the fewest work hours in an average year—about 1,337.

However, we still get weary from work. There are many people today working full-time on the job and then working just as hard off the clock meeting their responsibilities at home.

Kim Bolton tells of a workday that many stay-at-home parents can relate to. She looked around at mounds of unwashed laundry and un-mopped floors, and she silently dedicated herself to a day full of cleaning. Just as she was getting into a cleaning rhythm, her two-year-old son called to her, "Hey, Mom—why dontcha come and sit wif me in da big chair?" Kim protested. She tried to explain how busy she was. She promised to sit with him later. But he continued to smile that charming smile and pat the chair next to him. Finally, Kim put down her laundry and settled into the chair with her son. The two of them snuggled for a minute or so—then her son patted her on the leg and said, "You can go now."

In a hectic day, he had insisted that she take just a moment to rest with him. He understood her busyness, but he also understood that their time together was more important to both of them. Bolton said that for just a moment, her two-year-old boy was an example of Jesus to her. "Come to me, all you who are weary and burdened, and I will give you rest. Take my yoke upon you and learn from me, for I am gentle and humble in heart, and you will find rest for your souls. For my yoke is easy and my burden is light" (Matthew 11:28-30).

Neil T. Anderson puts it like this:

> Jesus invites you to a restful walk in tandem with Him, just as two oxen walk together under the same yoke. "How can a yoke be restful?" you ask. Because Jesus' yoke is an easy yoke. As the lead ox, Jesus walks at a steady pace. If you pace yourself with Him, your burden will be easy. But if you take a passive approach to the relationship, you'll be painfully dragged along in the yoke, because Jesus keeps walking. Or if you try to race ahead or turn off in another direction, the yoke will chafe your neck, and your life will be uncomfortable. The key to a restful yoke-relationship with Jesus is to learn from Him and open yourself to His gentleness and humility.  📖

---

*David Graves is senior pastor of College Church of the Nazarene, Olathe, Kansas.*

# INVEST IN OTHERS

STEVE WILSON ·······························································

One of the most exciting decisions you can make is to be on the lookout for opportunities to invest in others. For me, this has been one of the most powerful principles in my life. Almost 30 years ago I was driving to Seattle from Spokane with Terri, my wife, to see her folks. I was listening to a Zig Ziglar tape and was deeply impacted when he said "You'll always have everything you want in life if you'll help enough other people get what they want." When I heard this statement, something changed inside me, and I made a decision: *I'm going to do it.* That decision to look for ways to help others, to invest in them, changed my life.

I believe that one of the marks of true greatness is to develop greatness in others. "There are three keys to more abundant living: caring about others, daring for others, and sharing with others" (William Ward). I have found that many great men and women often have a common perspective that greatness is not deposited in them forever but rather flows through them into others. "We make a living by what we get, but we make a life by what we give" (Norman MacEwan).

When we travel on business, our journeys are self-motivated by what we'll get in return for our trouble. But in the journey, might we also be able to see opportunities to simply help others without regard for what we might receive? Assign yourself the purpose of making others happy, and thereby give yourself a gift.

People have a way of becoming what you encourage them to be. Ralph Waldo Emerson observed, "Trust men, and they will be true to you. Treat them greatly, and they will show themselves great." Spend your life lifting people up, not putting people down. Goethe advised, "Treat people as if they are what they ought to be, and help them to become what they are capable of being."

There are two types of people in the world: those who come into a room and say, "Here I am!" and those who come in and say, "Oh, there you are!" How do you know if a man or woman is good? He or she helps to make others good. Find happiness by helping others find it. The Bible says it this way: "Knowing that whatsoever good thing any man doeth, the same shall he receive of the Lord" (Ephesians 6:8, KJV). A good deed bears interest. You cannot hold a light to another's path without brightening your own. ▮▮▮

---

*Steve Wilson is an NFL official and executive pastor of Spokane Valley Church of the Nazarene, Spokane Valley, Washington.*

# HE IS THE TRUTH

MONTY LOBB ∿∿∿∿∿∿∿∿∿∿∿∿∿∿∿∿∿∿∿∿∿∿∿∿∿∿∿∿∿∿∿∿∿∿∿∿∿∿∿∿∿∿∿∿∿∿∿∿∿∿∿∿∿

*For this reason I was born, and for this I came into the world, to testify to the truth. Everyone on the side of truth listens to me* (John 18:37).

How important do you think truth is to God? It must play a significant role, because Jesus told Pilate it was the reason He was born. Though we often assume Jesus' primary mission was to save the lost—He first had to testify to the truth.

Testifying to the truth paints a picture of a courtroom drama. As a lawyer, I know the judge and jury aren't interested in hearing various versions of the truth; rather, they're interested in having *the* truth revealed before them. It's more than ironic that in our culture the idea that there are multiple truths and that all are equally relevant is an idea that's supported and encouraged.

Maybe the popularity of competing truth claims is attractive because we don't like what the Bible's absolute truth says about our behaviors, attitudes, and thoughts. Quite possibly the Hollywood movie has it right when the colonel on the witness stand, in a derisive and patronizing manner, informs the military attorney that, he "can't handle the truth."

Can *we* handle the truth? Often we can't. Only with the help of the Holy Spirit (John 16:13) can we handle the truth. The truth isn't always pretty. It has consequences, makes demands, and causes us discomfort. The great thing about truth is that the Author of truth gave us His Son, whose primary purpose is to help us clearly see light from darkness and then walk in His light (John 3:21). Following truth will free us from lies, because the very nature of truth beckons us to be open, honest, and transparent with God, ourselves, and others.

But such freedom has a price. God's claims about himself and authentic life through Him are radically different from the messages of our culture, which tells us that there is no God, or that there is a God but that He is impersonal, or that we are God and the source of our own self-fulfillment. This cosmic battle is fought on the various frontlines of truth; thus, the truth that Jesus came to testify to demands that we either wholeheartedly believe Jesus or dismiss and doubt Him. Either way, our behavior confirms our position on the truth claims of Jesus.

What areas of my life, if I am truthful with myself, are causing pain to me, my family, friends, folks at work, and God? Use your travels this week to discern whether there are any areas in which you're hiding from the truth in your life. 📖

---

*Monty Lobb is the president of Kenosis Ltd.*

# RAGING AGAINST WISE JUDGMENT

RICK KARDOS ·····················································

*A man who isolates himself seeks his own desire; He rages against all wise judgment* (Proverbs 18:1, NKJV).

*When tempted, no one should say, "God is tempting me." For God cannot be tempted by evil, nor does he tempt anyone* (James 1:13).

Bud Searcy of One by One Ministries shares that "all sex addicts feel detached, isolated and alone." Loneliness can be acute when we are on the road. Temptation seems to be everywhere we turn. Proverbs 18:1 talks about the man who "willfully separates and estranges himself" (AMP.), which rightly describes where we live when we fall prey to sexual temptation. Our thoughts become self-centered and self-focused and we find ourselves in a conceited life, which leads to shame. This creates a vicious cycle, pulling us back to the unmanageable and damaging thoughts and behavior that caused us to become isolated in the first place!

James 1:13-15 reminds Christian men of their arrival in denial and rationalization to this vain life, desiring to be the center of attention even when alone. Verse 14 informs us of both the truth and the order of our sin. We are tempted *after* our desire has set in motion the lust of the eyes. When temptation then confronts our senses, we must decide: do we fall to our evil desires, or do we say no and refuse to entertain the temptation? Why? Entertaining but not acting on the desire is still sin. Stopping the behavior via self-will is only a temporary solution. Stopping habitual sexual sin requires His grace and the resultant heart-directed action. Entertaining and then using our own power to stop is simply "managing sin."

We must acquire wise counsel in the presence and words of our brothers in Christ. By humbly seeking their help, we decrease the chance of entertaining and succumbing to the desire—the lust of the eyes. Wise counsel can both prevent and help eliminate our habitually arrogant behavior. It will help us grow in Christ! We must choose rightly, as James teaches, heeding the warning of Proverbs 18:1 never to isolate—always asking for and taking wise counsel. ▮

---

*Rick Kardos is the executive director of National Coalition for the Protection of Children & Families in New England.*

# ARE *YOU* HURRICANE-READY?

WILLIAM MARSHALL DUKE ·····················································

I live in Cincinnati. From Galveston, Texas, that's 1,129 miles, or about 18 hours of driving. Cincinnati has snowstorms, drenching spring rains, scorching summer days, high humidity, occasional tornadoes. Hurricanes? They worry those living near water! They're headlines on The Weather Channel. I live in the Midwest. Hurricanes? That's just an evening news story.

Well, that's the case most of the time, but not on Sunday, September 14, 2008!

Throughout the previous week, the country watched the progress of Hurricane Ike. Most of us Americans shook our heads sadly as we watched folks from Houston to Galveston nail plywood over their windows, bundle their prized possessions into vehicles, and head for safer ground. Boy, was I glad that I was safe and sound!

Cincinnati meteorologists explained that due to Hurricane Ike, we would probably notice increased winds and maybe some rain on that Sunday afternoon. Nobody dreamed that such a broad swathe of midwest America would be rocked with wind gusts in excess of 80 miles per hour.

Trees collapsed, shingles took flight, plants were literally sucked out of the ground, siding was ripped off, vehicles were blown *over*, and power lines snapped. A huge chunk of the Midwest was immediately bathed in darkness, a darkness that for some would last over eight days as energy companies strained to recover from the phenomenon. People scrambled for candles, searched for generators, hunted for cell phone car-chargers, checked propane for the grill, and wondered what they would do without their electronic *necessities:* television sets, computers, and microwave ovens. And what about food?

We were unprepared for what transpired. What everyone was sure would never happen *did.* We had been lulled into a false sense of security. Hurricane Ike's winds wreaked havoc as they slammed the Midwest with unexpected fury.

Life can be like that as well. Satan cunningly tries to lull us into thinking we're in secure circumstances—our debts are paid, our bank account is solid, our stocks are growing, and we have steaks sizzling on the grill. We begin to treat our relationship with Christ with casualness: skipping morning devotions, uttering heartless prayers, diving into meals without thanking God for His blessings, missing worship services, lingering in front of television programs with questionable storylines, doing double-takes at the huge pictures of partially-clad females on the mall windows. Satan feeds us a line of normalcy, and we swallow it hook, line, and sinker. Before we know it, we're in the midst of a personal hurricane.

Peter and Paul, two stalwarts in the faith, deliver passionate warnings regarding the unsuspecting hurricanes that Satan injects into our lives. Peter pleads, "Keep a cool head. Stay alert. The devil is poised to pounce, and would like nothing better than to catch you napping" (1 Peter 5:8, TM). Paul warns, "God is strong, and he wants you strong. So take everything the Master has set out for you, well-made weapons of the best materials. And put them to use so you will be able to stand up to everything the Devil throws your way. This is no afternoon athletic contest that we'll walk away from and forget about in a couple of hours. This is for keeps, a life-or-death fight to the finish against the Devil and all his angels" (Ephesians 6:10-12, TM).

How about you? Are you alert and ready so that on the day when Satan encircles you with a hurricane, you'll be able to stand strong? Better check your armor, for certainly a storm is brewing! 📖

---

*William Marshall Duke is the coordinator of Men's Ministries for the Church of the Nazarene.*

# REJECTING PASSIVITY

**SEAN MCKAY** ·······················································

I've been married to my wife, Becky, for 12 years now. I'll be the first to admit that the first two years were filled with arguments, disagreements, and immaturity on both our parts. I later realized that no matter the situation—right, wrong, or indifferent—it was on me to do something about it.

I've been known as one who doesn't mind confrontation or saying what needs to be said. But in an argument with my wife recently, it came to a head when I understood that as the head of the household, I had the responsibility not only to not let the sun go down with anger between us, but also to be the one to reject passivity in all situations and reconcile with my wife.

That's easier said than done for most men, and for me it involved a lot of humility. You see, it's one thing to reject passivity when needed or when asking for forgiveness, but it's another to do it with compassion and humility. Either way, it needs to be done more often. I always advise husbands to remember 1 Peter 3:7—"Husbands, in the same way be considerate as you live with your wives, and treat them with respect as the weaker partner and as heirs with you of the gracious gift of life, so that nothing will hinder your prayers."

While I do not look at my wife as a weaker person, nor did Peter claim this to be a "look-down-upon" verse for wives or women, we're to protect and look out for our wives. This should be done with consideration, compassion, and mostly with tact.

We're called to have relationships that are right with others and our spouses. If we have a problem that might hinder our prayers, we should take the problem to those it concerns. Nathan did it with David, Paul did it with Peter, and we should carry it ourselves not only with our spouses but in all other relationships as well. Matthew 5:23-25 encourages us to go as soon as possible to settle matters quickly.

Reconciliation can be a powerful step for any relationship, but it takes a person of humility and a person who rejects passivity to get it done.  ▮▮▮

---

*Sean McKay owns his own business in Cincinnati, Ohio.*

# POWER OF WORDS

JEFF PRATHER ·······················································

Shakespeare writes, "Beware the stories you tell yourself, for you surely shall be lived by them." This has become a principle that greatly guides my work in counseling. For example, what we tell our children about who they are and what is important in life has a powerful impact. The stories and beliefs we give them, whether intentionally or not, tend to become internal guides for our children, greatly determining their sense of worth and their outlook on life.

In considering fathers who are quite busy or frequently travel away from family yet want to have an impact on their children's lives, I thought of how helpful it could be to consider the impact that words have had on our lives. Maybe we remember those who helped shape us. We may recall an occasion when a parent, teacher, or coach said something we would not forget, or we may have received certain messages over and over again. If we consider this truth of how words have impacted us, perhaps we'll learn to interact with our children with more awareness.

In working in counseling with fathers who are at times away from their families, it has become clear to me that they often feel less able to affect what's happening at home. Yet what I've found with these situations is that although it's ideal to have a father continually present, it *is* possible to connect and guide children while the father is away from home. For this to occur, it is key to focus on the child *before* and *when* you interact, considering such things as the joys or sorrows the child may have faced that day, or things he or she needs to do. How powerful it is for a father to demonstrate that he knows who his child is and that he wants to guide his children! The father who calls home distracted or irritable is sending a message to his child, intentional or not. In the same way, so is the father who calls and asks with interest about school, time with friends, and obedience to Mother.

Words *do* something. They create something. They are in part creating our children. Expressions of love, plus the effort to guide through one's words, directly help build esteem and abilities. I know a woman who at 79 years old still laments that her father never told her he loved her. I've watched the faces of kids in counseling as their fathers, who to that point have neglected verbal affirmation, share with them what they value about them. These experiences have reinforced for me that when I get it right, when I laugh with my sons, kiss them, and tell them about God, it meets a deep need for everyone involved. I have learned that calling home and talking to my boys can be a valuable time of speaking words of love and affirmation that strengthen the bond between us.

Increase your focus on your children. See your time with them not simply as fun or stressful but also as opportunities. As intimidating as it is, the fact is that we are co-creators with God of our children. Whether parents are aware or unaware of their position, the impact still exists. ▮▮▮

---

*Jeffrey W. Prather is a psychologist specializing in children and families.*

# PEACEMAKER

JOE WHITE ·······························································

*Submit to God and be at peace with him; in this way prosperity will come to you* (Job 22:21).

If there were a Heisman Trophy for high school football in Pennsylvania, it would have gone to Jim Schaunessey—at least in the football-savvy town of Oil Trough, where "Jim Schaunessey Day" is celebrated annually, even though his high school days are long-since behind him. If a player can succeed by being mean, tough, angry, and motivated by hatred, Jim was. Beaten severely by his dad regularly made Jim shoe-leather tough. "My dad would paint the kitchen with my blood," Jim recalls. "And then he would beat up my mom before my eyes."

Jim had one hiding place to run to when his dad was drunk and abusive. When his father found it, he kicked Jim until he was black and blue. Jim's outlet for his hatred was smash-mouthed football, and he earned a full scholarship to Arizona State University and eventually was drafted by the New England Patriots. "I was in hundreds of barroom fights," Jim now recalls matter-of-factly. "I never lost one."

During Jim's junior year in college, his life changed drastically when he met our crucified and risen Savior and used those three nails to pin his anger resolutely and permanently on that same Roman cross. Jim was a new man!

His second dramatic event was almost as big as the first. My friend Gary Smalley met Jim shortly after his conversion and challenged him to forgive his dad and go home to seek reconciliation. When Jim flatly refused, Gary said, "Jim, how much of your broken relationship with your dad is your fault?" Jim snapped back, "Three percent at most. Ninety-seven percent is my dad's fault."

Gary persisted. "As a follower of Christ, Jim, take 100 percent responsibility for your 3 percent." It made sense. Jim went home, where he was met with his father's typical obstinacy and ridicule. He took his aging dad behind the house and sought his forgiveness. Gallantly, Jim apologized for everything he had done to his dad. His dad responded harshly. Jim began to weep and pray with his eyes affectionately heavenward. *God, my Father, I just ask that someday my dad can know you as his Father as you have allowed me to know you.*

To Jim's surprise, his dad began to weep. This broken, bitter, and beleaguered man began to pray, *God, someday will you let me know you the way Jim does?*

God granted his request. Like a caterpillar changing into a butterfly, Jim's dad became a brand-new creation, and for the first time in his life he began to experience peace. The two walked as friends the remaining 14 years of his dad's life. They prayed together, played together, and traveled together to places his dad had always wanted to see. On his dad's deathbed, Jim fondly reaffirmed his tender love for him and released him to join his mom in heaven. The reconciling blood of Christ, which reinstated humanity (those who surrender to Christ) to a right relationship with God, had once again empowered two men in conflict to give each other the same priceless gift of reconciliation.

How is Christ calling you to be an agent of reconciliation in your world?

---

*Joe White is co-president and co-owner of Keanakuk Camps.*

# THE THREE RS OF RECOVERY

RICK KARDOS ·······················································

*Dear friends, I urge you, as aliens and strangers in the world, to abstain from sinful desires, which war against your soul* (1 Peter 2:11).

This spring my wife and I took a mini-vacation to Maryland and Washington, D. C., as a break from our ministry to families confronted with issues of sexual addiction and their recovery. As always, on Sunday we planned to visit a local church.

Expecting a blessing, we chose Frederick Christian Fellowship, with Pastor Randy Goldenberg. In the bulletin we read, "The Pillar of Recovery!" Pastor Goldenberg's message was the "Three Rs of Recovery." The central recovery issue? Sexual immorality, including addiction and pornography.

Before I share Pastor Randy's Three Rs, ask yourself a question. Who are you in Christ? You may not be a sexual addict, but more than likely you have experienced significant struggles with sexual issues, as all men have. You're blessed that the answer is profoundly given in the Three Rs!

**Reclaim the life God gave you** (1 Peter 2:9-10). As the scripture in 1 Peter reminds us, we are a chosen people, belonging to God, receiving salvation through His mercy. We are fallen people and will be in recovery the rest of our lives. A Bible scholar once said, "His forgiveness of our sins is not the end—rather, it is the beginning of the crisis of convalescence." Anti-developmental forces are meant to slow you down, to defeat you and keep you from recovery. The choice is yours to accept His gift, to be the royal priesthood He created you to be. We must reclaim the life we received through salvation.

**Remove the dark forces that robbed you** (Colossians 3:5-10). The anti-developmental forces are not permanent! Many are listed in Colossians 3, along with the admonition that you must remove them and put them to death. And rid yourself of the behaviors that accompany these forces. You have been renewed by Him. Your old self is gone. By His grace you can choose to *remove* the "forces" that rob you!

**Restore the worship God meant to sustain you** (Romans 12:1-2). Sunday is only a small part of worship designed by the Lord. His plan for worship is a Monday-through-Sunday, 24/7 time to enjoy His love and to share the same. We do this not only with words but also by action! We offer ourselves as a living example of His choosing us, sharing our renewal through His Word, allowing the transformation of our hearts to be visible to all.

Reclaim. Remove. Restore. Colossians 3:1 tells us that "since, then, you have been raised with Christ, set your hearts on things above." Because of Him, we can do it!   📖

---

*Rick Kardos is the executive director of National Coalition for the Protection of Children & Families in New England.*

# BLESSED ARE THOSE WHO LOSE

THOMAS SHEPHERD ·····································

*Give to everyone who asks you, and if anyone takes what belongs to you, do not demand it back* (Luke 6:30).

It was a sad, dreary day as I climbed into my car for the 90-minute drive home. A dramatic collapse against an inferior team had set my weary tail firmly between my legs. So I searched for something comforting on my iPod. Up several points toward the end of the match, I had let my mind stray to the embarrassment I would feel if I, well-known in the region as a former national squash champion, were to lose to the hometown favorites. And then, shot by shot and point by point, fear took over as I stumbled and chunked my way to defeat. To what could I attribute this stunning collapse? To what could I attribute this fear?

As I was considering these questions and listening with half an ear to the message on my iPod regarding Luke 6:17-36, I was struck between the eyes with Jesus' words. As paraphrased by the teacher, "Blessed are those who are weak, blessed are those who suffer, blessed are those who grieve, blessed are those who are excluded.

But woe to those who are powerful, woe to those who are comfortable, woe to those who are successful, and woe to those who are respected."

What struck me so powerfully was that I could relate far more easily to the conditions that bring woe than to those that bring blessings. And having just that morning tasted a rare, albeit mild, meal of suffering, weakness, and grief, I had absolutely no sense of the blessing of which Jesus spoke. President of my family business, former national champion squash player, beautiful family, beautiful home, plenty of money, good health, access to all the right people—and yet things in my life were not good. My marriage did not approach the intimacy that God designed for us, and my wife sensed it deeply. My relationship with my dad, who was also my boss, was severely damaged by my clumsy efforts to wrest control and right the ship that is our family business. What friends I had were largely established to check the ministry box, unless, of course, I could use the connection in some way for my benefit. And most disturbing was the fact that my relationship with Jesus was shallow and dry.

When Moses came down from Mount Sinai, he did not deliver God's Ten Commandments as a means of salvation as is the common misunderstanding. The Israelites had been rescued from slavery in Egypt well before the commandments were delivered. Rather, he delivered the commandments as a means to community. Have no other gods before me, remember the Sabbath, honor your mother and father, do not commit murder, and so on. Obedience to these commandments brings community, not salvation.

Likewise, Jesus' teaching at the base of the mountain in Luke 6 was also a means to community. And He was speaking directly to me. The teacher continued: "It is not that Jesus exhorts us to *seek* suffering, exclusion, weakness, and grief. Rather, we are to *prize* them as conditions that make His love for us and our community with others all the sweeter. And it is not that we are to *refuse* power, recognition, comfort, and success. Rather, we are to *be suspicious* of them."

I recognized on that car ride home that power, recognition, comfort, and success controlled me in a deep and profound way. Pride had its claws in me and was wrecking my relationships. As I responded defensively to comments that challenged my sense that I was noble, capable, and blameless; as I worked to manage how I appeared to others; as I avoided God's nudges to venture out into uncomfortable interpersonal encounters—I was letting pride steal from me the joy and full life that Jesus has for me in community with him and others.

With my drive home winding down, I recognized that it would take some time and lots of work to understand how I became this man who cooperated with the evil one to my own disadvantage. But it was easy to see where to start—on my knees and in God's Word—as I worked to renew my relationship with my Savior.

"Blessed are those who are weak, blessed are those who suffer, blessed are those who grieve, blessed are those who are excluded." In 30 years of competitive squash, I had never prized a loss as I did that day in my car.  📖

---

*Thomas Shepherd is president of Shepherd Chemical Company.*

# 'TIL DEATH DO US PART

DALE HARLOW ·················································

*Husbands, love your wives, just as Christ loved the church and gave himself up for her* (Ephesians 5:25).

Ephesians 5:25 is not nearly as well known as the one three verses earlier, which says, "Wives, submit to your husbands as to the Lord" (Ephesians 5:22). This verse is more controversial, because our society doesn't like the word "submit." Whenever the media hears that a political candidate is an Evangelical Christian, they ask about submitting. Most answer by dancing around it, knowing that if they claim to agree, it could seriously hurt them in the polls. But I don't think the command for wives to submit is nearly as difficult as the command for husbands to love their wives as Christ loved. At least submission is much more attainable.

Perhaps that's the point. God knows that men tend to be goal-oriented; after all, He created us. He knows that we conquer something and then move on to the next goal or achievement. So He gives us a goal that can never quite be achieved in this life—something to keep us busy permanently. We don't need to be frustrated by the fact we never fully attain it. We can always come closer.

So what exactly does it mean to love our wives as Christ loved the Church? It can be summed up in one word: sacrifice. What did Christ do for the Church? In case we missed it, the verse included it —He "gave himself up." He sacrificed.

Many men want to be the king of the house, not the servant. But Christ calls us to be something greater than a king. He calls us to be like the King of kings, by sacrificing.

Even women who think "submit" is a dirty word would love to be treated as Christ treated the Church. And maybe, just maybe, if we treat our wives that way, submission won't be so difficult.

When most men hear the word "sacrifice," they think of extremes. They think of giving their lives for someone else. Most men I know would die for their wives. But a bigger question might be—will you *live* for her?

Loving our wives as Christ loved the Church is the greatest challenge we could accept. You might be thinking, *You don't know my wife—she can be unbearable at times.* That may be true, but I do know that you accepted that responsibility when you said, "for better, for worse." You said, "I'm going to stay faithful regardless." Now, are you man enough to do it? Will you accept the responsibility?

What can you do today to show your wife that you love her and are willing to sacrifice for her? Make a commitment to act on at least one of those things each day this week. 📖

---

*Dale Harlow is senior pastor of Northfield Christian Church in Ft. Dodge, Iowa.*

# A DAD'S EXAMPLE

CHARLES DAVIS ·····································

*Love the Lord your God with all your heart and with all your soul and with all your strength. These commandments that I give you today are to be upon your hearts. Impress them on your children. Talk about them when you sit at home and when you walk along the road, when you lie down and when you get up* (Deuteronomy 6:5-7).

As a child and teenager, I was keenly aware of my father's lack of a formal education. Raised during the Great Depression, he obtained the equivalent of an eighth-grade education. He left school at an early age to take a job to help support his family. But he was a godly man, serving our local church in just about every capacity. However, when he got up to speak at church, his "educated" son winced at his grammar and lack of public speaking ability.

Over the years I have come to realize just how smart my father really is. You see, his is a storehouse of wisdom rather than facts, grammatical techniques, or trained skills. From him comes a sincerity and love that's not capable of being described in the textbooks. And he has been one of the most effective teachers I've experienced in all my years of formal education. Yet he has never even delivered a single lecture.

By example, my dad has taught me the love of God, family, and others. His devotion to God's Word has been exemplary. As a child and teenager, I regularly saw my dad seated in the living room chair by the table with the lamp, reading his Bible. Now dad was not a strong reader—he read in a whisper, mouthing out each word. Furthermore, for most of those years he was reading the King James Version.

I knew it was a struggle for him to understand the English of 1611. But over the years he never tired of reading each night.

When he turned 75, I asked him how many times he had read through the Bible. I knew he kept track of things like that. He told me he had records to show that he had read through the Bible 29 times. I still marvel when I think of that discipline. But I rejoice that my father modeled for me the *importance* of God's Word. I've never doubted that my interest and commitment to the study of the Word of God is, in large part, influenced by my father's example.

When I consider the impact my father has had on my life, I pray that my children have seen in me something of the character and commitment that I've witnessed in my father over the years. His wisdom truly is founded on his fear and love of God. In him I have seen the love of God expressed sacrificially in tangible ways to family, friends, and those in need. His character has been modeled so vividly that I cannot escape the influence he has had on me.

Now he is ill, and sometimes he does not know who I am. He's not able to read his Bible or attend church. But when the family gathers to eat, as cognitively disoriented as he is, he prays as somebody who personally knows the One to whom he is speaking.

Are you dedicated so much to Scripture that even when you're on the road, your children know without a doubt that you're still reading His Word?   ▯▮▯

---

*Charles Davis is an appeals court judge for the State of Florida.*

# SEXUAL PURITY: SPECIAL CHALLENGES WITH TRAVEL

DAVID MIDDENDORF ·················································

*God did not call us to be impure, but to live a holy life. Therefore, he who rejects this instruction does not reject man but God, who gives you his Holy Spirit* (1 Thessalonians 4:7-8).

I have a sticker on my motorcycle helmet that reads, "Lord, help me to be the man my dog thinks I am." Those of us with dogs know that our dogs think we're the greatest people on earth. My wife, Sharon, and I travel extensively on our Harleys and have to put Speck in boarding while we're gone. We feel guilty for leaving him, especially on long trips. I would not be surprised one day to find that as I pick him up from the kennel, he has decided that he doesn't want anything else to do with me. But every time I go to the kennel to bring him home after a trip, he greets me with the kind of joy only a guilt-ridden dog-owner can appreciate.

If only it were that easy to be focused and excited about living a holy life, especially when we're alone and away from home. This world we live in seems to set traps for us at every turn—traps designed to pull us away from the holy life we've been called to. Check in to most hotels and turn on the television set, and you're bombarded with offers to make your stay an exciting adventure. Many of these adventures are geared for men who are alone and away from home. Many hotels offer a manager's reception, in which guests are invited to mix and mingle with other guests in an atmosphere usually lubricated with light snacks and free beer, wine, or cocktails.

After a hard day of sales on the road, standing in a booth in the exhibit hall of a trade show, or working at a conference where you've either been presenting or been presented to, you're bone tired. You've been nice and friendly to people all day. It's time someone was nice and friendly to you. The town and the hotel you're staying in are prepared to meet any need you might have at any time. All you have to do is respond to the invitations. It could not be easier. You say, "I'm strong. I'm sure of my spirituality. I just need to relax—I've earned it."

Friend and brother, trust me—at this point in your day, if you're having to build up your spirituality to justify what you're being tempted to do, think again. When these situations happen and you find yourself moving in a direction you know you should not be moving in, stop and pray for the strength to move in a different direction. The Holy Spirit will honor your need, and you'll be strengthened in your walk at that moment. I don't write this as one who has not been tempted but as one who fights a constant battle and knows how our Lord responds to the cries of His children in times of temptation. Test Him on this—He won't fail you.

As Horatio R. Palmer wrote, "Ask the Savior to help you, comfort, strengthen, and keep you. He is willing to aid you; He will carry you through." 📖

---

*David Middendorf is the president of Uncaged Outreach Ministries.*

# DO YOU REALLY WANT YOUR PRAYER LIFE TO CHANGE?

GARY MATTHEWS·····················································

Does God seem so big that you feel you can't really approach Him? Is He like some dignitary or politician or entertainer whom you can't even talk to without having the right connections or enough money to buy your way to him or her? Is this why we pray so little and yet seek the advice of others so often? Or is it because we don't have the patience to wait for an answer in someone else's—make that God's—time frame? Are we that selfish, that we have to be in control of when we have to have a response? Or are we afraid of the response we might get because it may not be what we have in mind in our own little agenda of things?

Do any of these questions sound like something you might say or think, or do they hit a nerve you haven't been willing to admit to? Well, if they do, welcome to life in the fast pace of the 21st century.

Prayer is active communication. It happens to be between two individuals—you and God. It's really a voluntary submission to a dialogue. And a dialogue must engage both individuals. Prayer takes time out of your schedule as does any worthwhile activity. To pray requires action.

To pray to God requires a commitment on your part. God has already given His commitment to listen to you. As it says in 1 Peter 3:12, "The eyes of the Lord are on the righteous and his ears are attentive to their prayer." When you pray to God, you need to do several things. You need to get ready—move some things out of the way, set aside some time, remove yourself from interruptions— things you would do for a good friend or associate you desire to have a chat with. Learn to say to God what you need to say, and even go so far as to jot down notes. After all, you wouldn't want to forget to say something to your associate or boss or waste his or her time with endless words for fear he or she may not give you any time the next time you approach him or her. Real prayer is not just a litany of words tied together into beautiful-sounding phrases. Remember Christ's strong words about the prayers of the Pharisees in Matthew 6:5. After all, you just happen to be talking to the only omniscient individual in the universe. As Christ went on to say in verse 8, "Your Father knows what you need before you ask him."  📖

---

*Gary Matthews is a general contractor residing in Snohomish, Washington.*

# GOD THE FATHER

MONTY LOBB ·····················································

*If you, then, though you are evil, know how to give good gifts to your children, how much more will your Father in heaven give good gifts to those who ask him!* (Matthew 7:11).

I don't know about you, but I'm the type of person who becomes amazed on a fairly regular basis with the way objects work or with the stunning beauty of nature. My sense of wonderment comes from an appreciation and curiosity of how something was created. And although I almost never understand where my fascination comes from, I love the fact that God created me to enjoy things that I can't understand. So it is with the love of our Heavenly Father.

If there's one aspect of my faith relationship that needs continual improvement, it's deeply trusting the God of the universe to love me intimately. How can we trust something or someone by which we're amazed and which we appreciate—but can't rationally understand?

Maybe the best way of answering this ageless question is to use our belief in what we can see to inform our faith. For example, in wrestling with the love of God for me, I have a much better understanding of it when I consider my love for my children or reflect on my earthly father's love for me. When I watch my children sleep at night or feel them hanging around my neck, I sense a love for them I can't explain.

To think God's love for me is greater than the love I have for my children is mind-boggling. But His love is also trustworthy, because I choose to believe it's better than my own great love for my children. Or I can look at another trustworthy experience: the love shown by my earthly father. When I think of all the times he has loved me even when I didn't deserve it, and when I consider the countless examples of his sacrifices for me, I'm humbled. To believe God loves me more unconditionally and sacrificially than my dad does gives me hope and courage to trust Him.

What area of your life would benefit from a deeper level of trust in the Father? What needs to happen for that to occur?   📖

---

*Monty Lobb is the president of Kenosis, Ltd.*

# LEADING COURAGEOUSLY

ERIC BOLES ·········································································

*God did not give us a spirit of timidity, but a spirit of power, of love and of self-discipline* (2 Timothy 1:7).

I love stories about courageous men. One story I particularly love is from the book *The Lakota Way*, which describes the men of the Lakota tribe, known as some of the greatest warriors of all time. They were feared in battle. Every young man was raised to be a warrior for the tribe.

Within the tribe was a small group of men called the "Red Shirt Warriors." They were the best of the best, a prestigious club that every young warrior strove to be a part of. The color red in the Lakota culture stood for honor. They always wore something red into battle to let the other warriors know where they were and to follow their lead. It is said that when battles appeared extremely difficult, the Red Shirt Warriors would dismount their horses and stake themselves to the ground, sending a message to their brothers and their enemies that they would die if necessary and would fight and not run.

As men of God, we're warriors as well. We may not be wearing red shirts, but we're covered in the blood of Jesus Christ. We can stand as Paul calls us to do in Ephesians 6. Our wives, our children, our brethren, and our churches need us men to stake ourselves to the ground and stand, letting everyone know we're here to fight and will not run.

There are times I've fled, retreated, and conveniently taken the path of least resistance. I've hidden behind excuses like Moses, blamed the woman in my life for my circumstances like Adam, scammed my way into opportunities like Jacob—and despite all that, God has forgiven me. He has restored me and reminded me that I'm more than a conqueror (Romans 8:37). I am a Red Shirt Warrior, covered in the blood of Jesus Christ.

In your place of work, do you stand uncompromising in the ways of God, sending a message to all around you of your commitment to His way?  ▮▮

---

*Eric Boles is cofounder of Diversified Learning Partners.*

# THREE QUESTIONS

J. K. WARRICK ··············································

*Is it well with you? Is it well with your husband? Is it well with the child?*
(2 Kings 4:26, NKJV).

When I was a kid, we played a game called "Twenty Questions." I don't remember all that much about the particulars, but I do remember playing. I have a friend who seems to teach more by asking the right questions than most people can teach when they give answers.

The prophet Elisha had some friends in the town of Shunem. They became very close, and soon the couple built a room for the prophet to use when he passed through the area. This couple had no children and wanted a family. Elisha realized how important this was to them, and God gave them a son.

One day while with his father in the fields, the boy suffered a severe illness and died rather quickly on his mother's knees. She placed him on the bed in the prophet's chambers and set out to find Elisha. As she approached him on Mt. Carmel, he sent his servant to greet her with three questions. You can read the rest of this wonderful story in 2 Kings 4:8-37.

For today, I want us consider the three questions:

*Is it well with you?* John Wesley insisted that those who came to faith in Jesus Christ join small groups of other believers in which they were continually asked this kind of question. Is it well with you today? How about your thoughts, words, actions, desires, responses, plans, possessions, passions, pursuits? Are they in keeping with who you say you are in Christ Jesus?

*Is it well with your wife?* Do you know how she is today? Do you know how she is emotionally, spiritually, physically, intellectually? Do you know how she's really doing? Are you listening to her? Are you looking for ways to show her how much you love and cherish her? What have you done today to let her know that you're thinking about her while you're away from home?

*Is it well with the children?* Will you call the children today? How will they know you're thinking about and praying for them? How are they really doing in school, in relationships, in their walk with Christ? What kind of habits are they developing? Do you know what sites they visit on their computers? What about their cell phones? What are their friends like?

Three questions—good questions. Perhaps it would be a good thing to meditate on these three questions for the next three days.

Today—how is it with you?

Tomorrow—how is it with your wife?

The day after—how is it with your children?

Prayer: *Heavenly Father, today give me grace to love deeply and to share openly. In Jesus' name. Amen.*

---

*J. K. Warrick is general superintendent of the International Church of the Nazarene.*

# WIVES AND HUSBANDS

SID BARTON ·····································

*Husbands, love your wives, just as Christ loved the church and gave himself up for her* (Ephesians 5:25).

To be perfectly honest, the admonition of Ephesians 5:25 scares me. To think that I may be called to the same level of sacrifice for my wife as Christ gave for the Church makes me wonder if I can possibly achieve this level of commitment.

I recall on my wedding day how it really hit me when the pastor asked if I would pledge before God and the witnesses gathered there to "take this woman, for better or worse, for richer or poorer, in sickness and in health, till death do us part." Frankly, I was scared by the realization of the level of commitment expected.

Clearly, anyone who has been married for any length of time has experienced the ups and downs that naturally occur between two imperfect people. Given this situation, why does God call us men to remain steadfast and committed? Obviously, I cannot speak for God, but I can relate my own experience of having been married to the same wonderful woman for 37 years and suggest the reasons this makes sense.

I think most of us would agree that a solid family with a committed, monogamous relationship between father and mother provides the best environment for children. I have seen the devastating effects of divorce and infidelity on the lives of children. The traditional family unit is the bedrock of our society and of God's plan for us.

But to be quite honest, having such a high standard of behavior for a man in the marriage relationship provides him with an opportunity to feel a sense of value and worth that cannot be found in any other endeavor in life. The sense of pride and fulfillment I feel in taking care of my wife and remaining committed to her is something that I cannot find anywhere else. Whenever times get tough and I'm tempted to look elsewhere for satisfaction, I think about the sacred vows I took so long ago, and I'm reminded of how important they are to me, my family, and my relationship to God. Through the help of the Holy Spirit, when I resist temptation and reinforce my commitment, God compounds my happiness and gives me peace.

I pray for strength and courage to continue to fulfill my marriage vows and that all of us Christian husbands will find the fulfillment that comes with this pledge. ⬛

---

*Sid Barton is the director of the management department for the Business School of the University of Cincinnati.*

# REMEMBER WHO YOUR LIFE IS!

KERRY W. WILLIS ·····················································

*When Christ, who is your life, appears, then you also will appear with Him in glory* (Colossians 3:4).

Is it me, or do we men seem to suffer from spiritual memory loss all too often? In fact, doesn't history support the idea that when we men choose to forget who God is, we immediately forget whose we are, and finally we even forget who we are?

Consider two Old Testament men as evidence that men can surely struggle with spiritual memory loss: Samson and David. Their spiritual memory loss happened along the exact same line—the line of lust. Sadly, these two men are past proof and present warning that when lust is locked into our thoughts, God is locked out of our lives. Yes, lust is a sure-fire way for us to forget who God is, whose we are, and who we are.

Samson and David proved that if lust reaches the season of full-bloom in our lives, God becomes unreal. When I travel away from my family and my accountability networks are out of sight, how can I make sure my spiritual memory stays strong? What can I do when temptation comes and lust knocks? I can simply choose to remember "Who my life is." Indeed, I can simply exercise the desperate words that the songwriter penned: I can *cry out to Jesus!* I can go to him because He is profoundly my life! By remembering Christ is my life—rather than bringing cruel reproach on His name and brokenness to my life and to the lives of my loved ones—I can experience God's glory.

Samson and David both committed idolatry in the same way that Adam did. All three of them forgot *who God was, whose they were,* and *who they were.* Adam pioneered idolatry in Eden when he yielded to Eve's wants and forgot God's words. Likewise, Samson forgot God as he was lost in the lap of Delilah. And David locked in lust for Bathsheba and locked God out of his life. All three men thought no one would get hurt. But *everyone* got hurt! Psalm 51 is David's prayer for pardon and purity. Let it be prevention for our lives.

Men, I invite you to pray my personal prayer: *Lord, help me to remember that you are not to be first place in my life or even the center of my life. Lord, help me to remember that you* are *my life! I plead the blood of Christ, who is my life! In your name I pray. Amen.*  💼

---

*Kerry Willis is vision pastor of Harrisonburg First Church of the Nazarene, Harrisonburg, Virginia.*

# WHAT GETS YOUR ATTENTION?

PAUL RADER ·······················································

I don't know how much you remember from your college days. A lot of it fades from the mind over time. But some statements from those years have lodged themselves indelibly in my memory.

E. Stanley Jones was an alumnus of my alma mater, Asbury College. He was a global evangelist and author of a score of devotional books when I was a student. During one of his frequent visits to our campus, I heard him preach in chapel on the theme "Whatever gets your attention gets *you*." I've never forgotten it.

We're immersed in imagery and ideas. Colorful and captivating images vie for our attention. So much of it is unavoidable. Those who create those images are determined to do all they can to ensure that we cannot ignore them. We all expend a great deal of mental and emotional energy sorting out what's worth our attention. There's no shortage of information, visual or otherwise. The skill we require is the ability to sort out what we can or can't afford to let grasp our attention. When we're on the road by ourselves, we suddenly become sensitive to the images that we have trained ourselves to avoid in our more familiar surroundings.

I believe in the value of filters that can spare us and our youth from exposure to images that are insidiously corrupting. Efforts to control access to Internet pornography sites, for example, are critical in protecting our families. Internet service providers should be the first line of defense. Other downloadable filtering options are available for the individual computer. These filtering strategies are all valuable. But ultimately, given the sheer ubiquity of images impacting us from multiple sources, filtering has to be an exercise in personal spiritual discipline. First Timothy 4:7 advises us to train ourselves to be godly.

The mind develops filters for sorting through the information it encounters. Norman Grubb comments that his own mind had become so Bible-soaked that it instantly rejected anything that did not square with the standards of scripture. For most of us, the problem lies in allowing so much information we ingest to evade the filters that we may have cultivated for discerning what is noble, pure, lovely, admirable, excellent, and praiseworthy (Philippians 4:8-9). Little by little, by carelessness or even courtesy towards those who may be watching with us, we become fascinated with images and ideas to which we soon become inured and that on reflection we know we ought to have rejected. What once might have made us blush now only elicits a sad chuckle. "Whatever gets your attention gets *you*."

We forget that God sees our computer screens and our TV monitors. Cutting off the right hand if it offends us is one thing, but exercising discipline in what we allow to be imprinted on our minds and memories—well, that's quite another! Whatever our rationalizations may be, we can be sure—"Whatever gets our attention gets *us*."   📖

---

*Paul A. Rader is a retired general in the Salvation Army.*

# TAKING A LITTLE TIME OFF

SCOTT PETERSON ·······················································

*When you fast . . .* (Matthew 6:16).

In Matthew 6 Jesus insinuates that fasting is going to be a part of our lives. He doesn't say "*If* you fast" but "*When* you fast." I'm not sure how it works for you, but for me fasting is difficult. While I've had periods in my life when I fasted, it's not one of those things that comes easily for me.

Yet in recent years I've come to understand that fasting is really about more than simply giving up food. Food is not the only thing that one can fast.

Even now as I write, I do so in the quietness of my office. I would love to write from home, but we have no electricity or water. You see, we had a major storm blow through our area last week, and in the process it took out trees and power lines. The people who are in charge tell me that it will possibly be more than a week before we get these things back. While they're things I want, it's interesting how life looks different when they're missing. The things that so easily crowd God out of my life are gone.

Times like this remind me that too often I allow music, television, videos, computer, e-mail, and countless other things to drown out the voice of God. These are a few of the things in my life that I need to give up for a period of time to allow God to speak clearly once again.

God wants to communicate with me, but sometimes all the noise and activity drown Him out. Sometimes I allow myself to become too dependent on other things. I think I can't live without television, a computer connection, electricity, and, of course, food or water. But somehow in those moments of struggle I realize that God needs to be first. It's God who ought to have control of my life. It's God who ought to be speaking into my life.

Maybe a few days without the necessities of life are actually good for me after all. Perhaps I should consider turning off the television set and the computer more often. Maybe days when I'm out of the office or on the road could be days for meditation, Bible reading, and prayer.

Giving something up reminds you of what really matters.  ▐▊▌

---

*Scott Peterson is the university chaplain at Mount Vernon Nazarene University.*

# PRAYER IN THE VALLEY

JOHN SPLINTER

In Psalm 23:4 David referred to "the valley of the shadow of death." Have you ever wondered what he meant by that? Was it his death? His child's? Did it have to do with clinical depression? His son's rape of his daughter? Or another son's coup attempt? Whatever the reason, the phrase says it all—"the valley of the shadow of death." Have you ever been there?

If you have, did you try to pray your way out of it? Did it work? If not, how did it change your faith? I ask this because it was in those agonizing, seemingly hopeless black moments that David observed one thing, and that one thing altered his understanding of both faith and prayer.

That one thing was God's presence. David wrote, "Even though I walk through the valley of the shadow of death, I will fear no evil, for you are with me." God's presence is the antidote to fear. It's our assurance in the darkness. We either believe that He has a plan and that His plan is good, or we succumb to fear, asking ourselves if God knows about our pain or even cares.

It is this sense of spiritual abandonment that often causes doubt. It's far easier to have faith and to pray when life is light and breezy—when there is no pressing need for faith—than it is when the only possible solution to a tragedy is God's personal intervention. Yet God in His providence sometimes allows life-bending horrors. Christ knew this.

These moments of darkness don't always fit well with our theologies of faith. So it was that Martha, speaking of her dead brother, Lazarus, said to Christ, "Lord, if you'd only been here, my brother wouldn't have died." Since she was speaking to Christ, we could call her comment a prayer. In one way or another, we've all prayed that prayer. It's a prayer of doubt, implying that God is not truly omnipresent, or else is not omniscient, or worse, might not be loving.

The apostle Paul addressed this doubt when he said, "I am convinced that neither death nor life, neither angels nor demons, neither the present nor the future, nor any powers, neither height nor depth, nor anything else in all creation, will be able to separate us from the love of God that is in Christ Jesus our Lord" (Romans 8:38-39).

Are you willing to get real with God and cry out to Him in your pain? If so, He is there.  📖

---

*John Splinter the executive director of National Coalition for the Protection of Children & Families in St. Louis.*

# A WIDOW'S GENEROSITY

BRUCE FONG ·····················································

Sometimes when we're traveling, those who surround us can be ministers of God's grace and love.

I was in Israel co-leading a tour following the footsteps of Jesus. Everyone who joined us on this excursion was excited. It's hard not to be enthusiastic when all of a sudden you find yourself walking the very land where Jesus walked.

We stood on the shores of the Sea of Galilee. Then we walked through the ruins of the town of Capernaum, the place where Peter lived and the site of much of what Jesus did in that region.

Then we set sail for a boat ride on the lake itself. Our minds rehearsed the calming of the sea, walking on the water, and casting the fishing net on the other side of the boat. We could see where Jesus likely delivered His Sermon on the Mount, multiplied the fish and bread, and cast out the demons from the man of Gadara.

It just seemed as if all of our senses were heightened. We could see with great detail. The sound of the wind was sharp and crisp. Fragrances made a memorable impression once in His land.

Everyone was on overload. There was too much to take in and much more to come. We gave the tour group a chance to reflect when we gave them free time to shop at a local merchandise shop.

What do you purchase as a memento for the trip of a lifetime? Some bought olive wood. Some selected beautiful local silk scarves. Others bought porcelain pieces decorated with images of Israel. Common products in a souvenir store became personal treasures for a lifetime.

One of our guests had a great idea. He asked the merchant for a widow's mite. The merchant gladly complied and brought out a sample. It was an oxidized simple copper coin so small that it was encased in a silver halo to make the coin stand out.

My interest in this keepsake grew. Then our guest asked how much the piece would cost. It was listed at one hundred five shekels. That translated into nearly 40 American dollars. For a coin whose value was only a fraction of a penny, it now had a modern-day equivalent value handsomely adjusted for inflation.

Jesus honored the gift of the widow. She gave out of her poverty, not out of her wealth. Her gift was representative of great personal sacrifice.

Giving is never about human value or quantity. God doesn't need worldly wealth. He's interested in our hearts as expressed with our giving. Generosity is a measure of our hearts, not what is printed on the calculator screen.

When you're traveling, consider the people and situations God brings across your path. New surroundings can be fertile ground for God's surprises.

Be encouraged in God's Word: Mark 12:41-44.   ▮▮▮

---

*Bruce Fong is president of Michigan Theological Seminary in Plymouth, Michigan.*

# THE LOVE OF GOD

JERRY KIRK ·······················································

Today let's focus our attention on the love of God in Jesus Christ for you and me. The people I know whose lives are the most blessed and who impact others most consistently are the people who are continually nurtured by the love of God in Jesus Christ.

The central message of the Bible is that God redeems us by faith in Jesus Christ and thereby makes us His dearly loved children (Ephesians 5:1-2). This truth transformed the apostle Paul's life and ministry. "I pray that you, being rooted and established in love, may have power, together with all the saints, to grasp how wide and long and high and deep is the love of Christ, and to know this love that surpasses knowledge—that you may be filled to the measure of all the fullness of God" (Ephesians 3:17-19).

As a pastor for more than 50 years, and having counseled with thousands of people, I have learned that when it comes to experiencing the love of God, we all have damaged receiving mechanisms. The deficiency is not in the adequacy of God's love, which is infinite, sacrificial, and constant, but in our capacity to believe and receive that love for ourselves on a continual basis.

Our receiving mechanisms have been damaged through harsh words and actions from parents, siblings, spouses, children, teachers, coaches, bosses, and friends. We have been damaged through broken relationships from criticism, rejection, abuse, abandonment, and unforgiveness, through personal failures, selfishness, pride, lust, and through not living up to our own expectations or those of others close to us. We have all damaged receiving mechanisms that hinder us from fully experiencing God's love.

In 1990 I decided that every time I saw a cardinal bird I would intentionally stop and thank God for His love in Jesus Christ. This daily reminder blessed me greatly. But in 1991 I took a giant step forward by deciding to expand the "remembrance trigger" to when I saw any bird. Since that day I have been reminded of God's love for me every day and during these intervening years hundreds of thousands of times. Every hour of every day for 17 years when I have seen a bird, I've thought of God and remembered His love for me in Jesus Christ, and I've given thanks and praise to God. My receiving mechanism is in process of being healed!

Will you join me today in asking and answering these personal questions? It's helpful if we do it in writing. What place does the love of Jesus Christ have in my life? How often do I think about His love for me and His love through me? How much does His love influence my thoughts about Him, my worship of Him, my joy in Him, my obedience to Him, and my desire to share Jesus and His love with others? Would it help me if I chose a "remembrance trigger," like the birds, flowers, or Mother Theresa's trigger of each person in need being Jesus?

---

*Jerry R. Kirk is the founder and chairman of the board for National Coalition for the Protection of Children & Families.*

# PRAYER IS ABOUT SPECIFICS

GARY MATTHEWS ·····································

Prayer is not carried on the back of clichés, nor is it rote repetition of words that served even some of the saints of old. Remember— Christ said in Matthew 6:8, "Your Father knows what you need before you ask him." So come boldly to God and do as directed in Hebrews 4:16—"Let us then approach the throne of grace with confidence, so that we may receive mercy and find grace to help us in our time of need." Why do we revere saints of old or some prayer warriors we may know? Because they go right to the very heart of God in their requests. They don't waste time reciting some great history or a bunch of phylacteries! Would you want to listen to millions of people reciting the same things without substance over and over?

When we get specific with God in what we pray, we actually begin the process of identifying what is important and necessary versus desirable or inconsequential. When we identify the important, we are probably getting closer to identifying what God's will actually is in most situations by stripping away the other trappings of life. And who knows—God may just bless us with some of our desires as a function of His great grace as He responds to solving our identified needs.

As you travel, think about what it is that you really need to pray. Try writing it down—really identify it so you can pray without being vague. What is it that interests you or is tweaking your heart? Ask, and try to answer the famous *who, what, why, when,* and *where* questions. You may be amazed at what you observe in the growth of your prayer life.

But be careful! God may answer your prayer, and that may change or even totally upset your life as you once envisioned it!

Do you mean it? Then pray it. ▮▮▮

---

*Gary Matthews is a general contractor residing in Snohomish, Washington.*

# ABOVE ALL ELSE, GUARD YOUR HEART!

BOB RECCORD ·······················································

*Above all else, guard your heart, for it is the wellspring of life* (Proverbs 4:23).

I was slated to speak in Orlando, Florida, to a conference of couples in leadership from all over the country. I was on the schedule for the next morning, and I had flown in the night before to hear a couple of my friends who were also on the program. For once I was able to soak in some great teaching just like everyone else in the audience!

Following a great evening, I retired to my hotel to relax before I had to deliver my own message the next morning. Lying back in bed, I was channel surfing—being brain dead for a few minutes before calling it a night.

Not much of interest was on, so I just kept surfing. Then suddenly and unbelievably came a sexually explicit scene. I couldn't believe it! This wasn't pay-for-view. Nor was it a movie. This was cable TV. My mind raced and struggled in shock at the same time. I quickly turned it off. I grabbed my Bible. I had been married more than 25 years. My marriage with Cheryl was strong. I was committed and contented. Yet even as I turned it off quickly and worked to focus my heart and think of Cheryl, in the back of my mind a voice said, *Turn it back on. You don't want to miss this. Besides, no one will ever know.*

There I was, preparing to speak the next day on "Guarding Your Heart and Home" and yet being tempted to leave my own heart unguarded the night before. And the temptation was *No one will ever know.* There's is a huge fallacy in that statement. Two people *would* know—Christ and I! How could I even think that I could speak to people the next day on guarding their hearts and marriages if there was compromise in my own life? And while people see us only externally, God looks way beyond that. He looks at the heart, below the waterline of our lives. And we can hide nothing from Him. What's more, He holds us accountable with what we do in our private moments as well as our public moments.

Because of making the right decision in private the night before, I was able to stand uncompromised before hundreds of couples the next day and challenge them to be on guard, because if we lose it in our hearts and homes, then we lose it all!

Remember—guarding your heart doesn't just happen. You have to make intentional, and often fast, decisions. And what you decide in private will determine your impact in public.    📖

---

*Bob Reccord is the president and CEO of Total Life Impact Ministries.*

# WIT'S END

JACK SCHRAND ·····················································

*Where can I go from your Spirit? Where can I flee from your presence? If I go up to the heavens, you are there; if I make my bed in the depths, you are there. If I rise on the wings of the dawn, if I settle on the far side of the sea, even there your hand will guide me, your right hand will hold me fast. If I say, "Surely the darkness will hide me and the light become night around me," even the darkness will not be dark to you; the night will shine like the day, for darkness is as light to you* (Psalm 139:7-12).

Relax—God is near. Have you ever felt that God is nowhere to be found when you seem to need Him most? We've all felt that way at times. Stop to think that these are the times when we grow as His men! As little boys, we needed to be given the opportunity to fail. When we passed the test, we puffed out our chest and said, "I did it, Dad!" This gave us confidence to tackle the next challenge when it came, and it surely did. If we were not regularly challenged, our growth toward manhood was also stalled. We need life's victories to grow, as men and as Christians. We also need to skin our knees a few times to learn how to get back up and get back into the fight.

They were at their wit's end. Then they cried out to the
LORD in their trouble, and he brought them out of their distress
*(Psalm 107:27-28)*.

These times are just as important. We need to realize that we
can't always do it on our own. We always need Jesus. We need to
quickly humble ourselves before God and confess, *I'm at my wit's
end. Please save me, Jesus!* Sometimes these tragedies occur because
we made wrong choices. This is where we need and appreciate
God's mercy and forgiveness. We can't hide from God in darkness.
He's just waiting for us to cry for help in being willing to repent.
Then God will take over. These are also the times when Christ builds
godly compassion in us towards others. Without recognizing our
own failings, we may not appreciate how important God's mercy to
others may be.

He has showed you, O man, what is good. And what does the
LORD require of you? To act justly and to love mercy and to walk
humbly with your God *(Micah 6:8)*.

As far as it applies to me, I must do and be just. As far as it applies to others, I must show God's mercy. Then I must confess that
none of this is possible except that God does this through me. Now
here's your challenge. Live Micah 6:8. Show your wife, your co-
worker, or even your competitor the same mercy you so desperately
need. Humbly let God live through you today. Be God's conqueror,
and let Him share His treasure with you. It's definitely worth it! Win
or lose, you can't go where God won't be with you. In the end you'll
always win with Jesus.  ▯▯▯

---

*Jack Schrand is a real estate salesman with Coldwell Banker West Shell: The Schrand Team in
Cincinnati, Ohio.*

# MARRIAGE: SERVICE TO ONE ANOTHER

DAVID MIDDENDORF ·············································

*There are different kinds of service, but the same Lord* (1 Corinthians 12:5).

My calling to full-time ministry to bikers, bars, and prisons was quite a change from how I had been serving the Lord. I was a minister of music and worship for a number of years in a mid-sized church in North Carolina. I called it a ministry of "maintaining the saints." My goal was to provide music to the congregation that would usher them into worshiping the Lord whom most of them knew and loved. My ministry had very little to do with reaching outside the walls of the church except during Christmas and Easter, when the C&E (Christmas and Easter) crowd made their twice-annual appearance to hear a cantata or see a dramatic presentation. Now I can count on one hand the number of Sundays I'm at my home church in a year.

I was a minister of music not because I was qualified but because I was willing. A large part of my being willing was knowing that Sharon, my wife and best friend, would be with me no matter what. Now that God has called me to minister outside the walls of the church to a very different congregation, Sharon is again right by my side doing whatever needs to be done and going whenever and wherever we're called to go.

When I was the minister of music, Sharon sang in the choir and often critiqued my leading or song selection, and not always in a way that sat well with me. Today we both ride Harley-Davidson motorcycles across the country, and just as in the choir, she sometimes critiques my leading and road selection—and not always in a way that sits well with me. I sometimes think I'm the one who has made the greatest change in ministry in my response to God's calling, but then I remember that God has not called Sharon—she has responded because she loves me and loves that I am where God wants me to be.

Sharon sacrifices her wants and needs to be with me in the calling that God has placed on my life. We're in this together, serving each other as we serve God. Sharon is giving herself up to serve God with me the same way that Christ gave himself up for the Church. As Paul writes in Ephesians, "Husbands, love your wives just as Christ loved the church" (Ephesians 5:25). I love my wife, and I love serving with her in the ministry God has blessed us with.

When I'm on the road and Sharon is not with me, I'm incomplete. Our service to each other is that we make each other complete in ministry and in life. Does that mean we agree on everything and think of each other as perfect in every way? Certainly not, but our marriage is not built or measured on perfection—it's built on our love for each other and our devotion to the calling God has blessed us with.

Are you and your spouse giving yourselves in service to each other the way Christ gave himself for the Church? Don't miss this blessing from the Lord on your marriage.  ▯▮▯

---

*David Middendorf is the president of Uncaged Outreach Ministries.*

# GODLY CHARACTERISTICS: A PERSONAL STORY

JOHN SPLINTER ·······················································

One summer evening after church when I was a boy, a friend and I invented games to play with a tennis ball while we waited for our parents to finish their conversations. It was fun to throw the tennis ball to one another over the lighted neon sign in the church's front yard—fun, that is, until my throw didn't quite make it over the sign and I broke one of the neon letters in "First Baptist Church."

The silence that followed was deafening. My dad, the visiting pastor, gave me the look that said, "You're dead meat." Then he ordered me to walk home to my grandparents' house—a half block away—and go to my room to wait for him. It was a very long half hour before he came home. I knew what was coming.

Downstairs I could hear my grandpa's voice and my dad's voice. Dad's voice sounded like a lion. Grandpa's was more gentle. The conversation went on for several minutes. Toward the end, the lion's voice seemed to soften. I didn't know what was happening until Grandpa came to my room and said, "Hey, little buddy—you're free to come out. Everything's okay."

In some translations of the Bible is found a word that's seldom used anywhere else but the Bible. The word is "propitiation" and has to do with the work of Christ on the Cross through which He satisfied God's wrath. Synonyms for propitiation might include terms such as "imputed righteousness," "indemnity," or "substitutionary atonement." In case none of those words ring any bells for you, here's a Bible verse that says it all:

> God presented Jesus as the sacrifice for sin. People are made right with God when they believe that Jesus sacrificed his life, shedding his blood. This sacrifice shows that God was being fair when he held back and did not punish those who sinned in times past *(Romans 3:25, NLT)*.

The concept of propitiation became clear to me on that summer's evening as my Grandpa stood between me and my angry father. Years later I learned that Grandpa paid for the repair to the sign—a cost that would have been impossible for me, a 7-year-old, to pay. He helped my dad's anger go away by paying the cost out of his own pocket.

Christ is your propitiation. In a curious sort of way, God provided the solution to His own wrath—wrath caused by our sin. That solution is Christ. So what does this tell you about God's character? If you were going to use three or four words to describe it, what would they be?   📖

---

*John Splinter is executive director of National Coalition for the Protection of Children & Families in St. Louis.*

# FATHERING

WOODIE STEVENS ·····························································

*These commandments that I give you today are to be upon your hearts. Impress them on your children* (Deuteronomy 6:6-7).

Recently I led a work team to New Orleans to help with restoration needed after Hurricane Katrina.

In New Orleans the young man behind the car rental counter said, "You know, they haven't fixed the levies yet. It's been seven months. The president says he's going to get us some money to fix them, but I don't know if he'll be able to. I really think people are just taking all that government money and sticking it in their pockets."

An image of the chaos and anarchy flooding New Orleans flashed through my mind. I replied, "Don't lie. Don't steal. Don't murder. Be true to your mate. It's the only way to a civilized society." The man looked at me as if he had never heard those concepts before.

The next week just two miles from my home a sheriff's deputy was shot to death. Standing at the post office a few days later, a lady behind me said to the postal clerk, "Have they caught that guy yet?"

"Not yet, but they will!" replied the postman.

I said, "Don't lie. Don't steal. Don't murder. Be true to your mate. It's the only way we can have a civilized society."

Sudden it got quiet in the post office. As the clerk handed me the stamps and my change, he mumbled, "Thanks for the advice."

The next week I heard someone tell of meeting a man in prison, and that prisoner's father was housed in the same prison. They had met each other for the first time in that jail. The younger man was a father also. He, too, had a son he had never met. He said, "The first time I will ever meet him will be in this jail."

Could I convince you? Don't lie, don't steal, don't murder. Be true to your mate. It's the only way to a civilized society.

I started saying that so much that my wife got tired of it. Then one morning she read these verses in Deuteronomy 6:5-7: "You must commit yourselves wholeheartedly to these commands that I am giving you today. Repeat them again and again to your children. Talk about them when you are at home and when you are on the road, when you are going to bed and when you are getting up" (NLT).

I told this story at a family camp. A few weeks later a mother who attended family camp e-mailed me. She wrote of sitting in her family room and turning to see their six-year-old daughter prance into the room announcing to all, "Don't lie, don't steal, don't murder, be true to your mate. It's the only way to a civilized society."

Children are listening and learning. You're teaching not only by what you say but also by how you live. Be faithful to these principles, even when you're on the road—when nobody is around to hold you accountable. The way you live every day can bring glory of God.

---

*Woodie J. Stevens is the director of Sunday School & Discipleship Ministries International for the International Church of the Nazarene.*

# THE EYES HAVE IT

BOB RECCORD ·························································

*I made a covenant with my eyes not to look lustfully at a girl* (Job 31:1).

I spend a lot of time in airports, traveling from one side of the country to another. And everywhere you look, you can't miss it: plunging neck lines, short shorts, pants that look spray-painted on. No wonder *USA Today* titled a lead article "Infidelity Is in the Air for Road Warriors," speaking of the danger of infidelity amidst the high amount of business travel today. What's a guy to do?

One thing he had better do is guard his eyes. And that has to be a practiced art. Frankly, the decision has to be made before a guy finds himself in the midst of such enticing environments. To wait until you're faced with the temptation is too late.

What's the big deal? Great question. The eye is the window to the soul. It's the gateway for what will nourish the soul or what stains and strains it. Every man totally controls this portal.

Pornography is disastrous and debilitating. It stains a man's soul and causes unreal expectation that no woman can meet in a normal relationship, where she has no airbrushing, makeup artists, stage lighting, or unending designer wardrobes. An image gets set in a man's mind—literally burned in chemically—that will return at inopportune times. The damage can be devastating.

A University of Florida study by Beatriz Avila Mileham determined that one-third of all divorces in America can be traced to online infidelity; a porn site leads to chat rooms, then liasions, and finishes in betrayal.

Men find it easily accessible, totally affordable, completely anonymous, and increasingly addictive. In fact, medical studies reveal that following Internet sexual arousal and release, the hormone dopamine spikes in the brain, resembling what the brain looks like on heroin. No wonder men get so hooked on porn.

Now is the time to draw your boundaries, and here are a handful of suggestions:

1. Carry a picture of your wife by your driver's license so that you see it every time you reach for your license for airport security.
2. Steve Arterburn suggests learning to have bouncing eyes. You "build a reflex action by training your eyes to immediately bounce away from the sexual, like the jerk of your hand away from a hot stove."
3. Either keep the TV set off in your hotel room, or go only to sports or news channels. Call home regularly.

If you want to be fit, work out. If you want to be sharp, keep studying. If you want to stay pure, intentionally guard your eyes! ▯▯

---

*Bob Reccord is the president and CEO of Total Life Impact Ministries.*

# THE MERGING OF MARRIAGE

GEORGE D. MCKINNEY ·············································

*For this reason a man will leave his father and mother and be united to his wife, and they will become one flesh* (Genesis 2:24).

Charles Shedd, a contemporary Christian writer, likens marriage to the merging of two independent streams of water, each of which has its own identity and peculiarities, its own power, thrust, and individuality. He says that at the point where these two streams merge will be turbulence—a rising spray as the two individual forces meet.

The noise of many waters will be encountered, for some conflict and some chaos will be present—but as the two streams continue to flow together, they become as one stream. There develops a beauty, a majesty, a bigness, a richness, and a fullness that never could be realized if each stream went its own way.

During the early years of union, turbulence is frequent. Conflicts arise, because each stream is striving to maintain its identity and not lose its own personality in the merger. However, as the years pass and the individuals mellow, a growing understanding and forbearance are experienced, a heightened joy of sharing, giving, and taking, and a willing exercise of patient waiting.

Thus, the coming-together of the two streams eventually becomes a beautiful, harmonic, majestic flowing where the two have become one.

This coming-together to become one flesh involves, first, the leaving of mother and father. This signifies the reordering of all prior primary relationships and the establishment of a new primary relationship between husband and wife. No human being, not even mother and father, can be more important or closer to either spouse than the other spouse. Secondly, the becoming one flesh requires that each spouse commit to faithfulness in the union. There must be a determination to stick together for better or worse.

When these conditions are met, God commands His blessing upon the union, and the two became one flesh. This union is spiritual, physical, and psychological. Thus, the coming-together of the two streams can become a beautiful, harmonic reality that reflects the union between Christ and His Church. "Therefore what God has joined together, let man not separate" (Matthew 19:6).

As you travel, be wary of anything that might pose a threat to the harmony of your covenant relationship. 🜨

---

*George D. McKinney is jurisdictional prelate and general board member of the Church of God in Christ, Inc., San Diego.*

# DON'T GAMBLE WITH YOUR FUTURE

**ALEX MCFARLAND** ·····················································

*Dishonest money dwindles away, but he who gathers money little by little makes it grow* (Proverbs 13:11).

Gambling has become a ubiquitous phenomenon in our nation. Online gambling has exploded in recent years, and many hotels now feature in-room gambling opportunities via their cable networks. Fuel and food have become secondary at convenience stores, with most corner markets serving mainly as outlets for the lotteries.

Sadly, even many Christians have been ensnared by the urge to gamble. Americans now spend $550 billion per year on gambling—more than is spent on books, films, and recorded music combined. It's estimated that each year 15 times more is spent on gambling than is donated to all churches.

It's true that the word "gambling" does not appear in the Bible. But Scripture does warn against the desire for instant gratification and the false promises of questionable schemes. It also warns against oppression of the poor. Gambling exploits the poor and perpetuates detrimental conditions that we can totally avoid.

Wise King Solomon warned against the desire for quick riches (Proverbs 28:20). Gambling discourages the principle of deferred gratification. In a culture that's already grossly self-indulgent, we would do well to remember that it's a virtue to be able to say no to ourselves. Gambling fosters a live-for-the-moment mentality. No matter what the falsely promised benefits may be, governments, individuals—and certainly Christians—are being incredibly shortsighted when participating in gambling.

But for the believer, more is at stake than just fiscal irresponsibility. Gambling compromises Christian stewardship and Christ's Lordship. The money we have is not our own to squander—it belongs to God and has been entrusted to us by Him. Further, Jesus Christ is entitled to have authority over every aspect of our lives, and succumbing to the gambling obsession is not honoring to Him.

Internal virtue on the part of citizens and favorable external conditions on the part of a society or an economy are required for true success and long-range growth. Gambling in any form erodes both. The record of history and Scripture both promise blessing and peace for those who stand with God and for what is right. And that's guaranteed. ▮▮

---

*Alex McFarland is president of Southern Evangelical Seminary in Matthews, North Carolina.*

# THE SERENITY OF STEWARDSHIP

NOEL BOUCHÉ ·······················································

*Unless the Lord builds the house, they labor in vain who build it; unless the Lord guards the city, the watchman keeps awake in vain. It is vain for you to rise up early, to retire late, to eat the bread of painful labors; for He gives to His beloved even in his sleep* (Psalm 127:1-2 NASB).

While 80 percent of the world's population lives on less than 10 dollars a day, hundreds of millions enjoy levels of wealth and convenience that were inconceivable only decades ago. Supermarkets provide food from across the globe; luxury goods are available to the masses; myriad forms of entertainment are accessible at the push of a button. Even middle-class incomes in developed economies can provide fabulous homes and tickets to travel the world.

But this affluence leaves us vulnerable to the twin evils of arrogance and anxiety, both of which are byproducts of the pride of ownership. In one moment, we arrogantly claim our possessions as our own and forget the Lord, who alone has provided us with resources (Deuteronomy 8:17-18). In the next moment, we're racked with anxiety. Whether it's market turbulence threatening our nest egg, the Joneses' new car pressuring us to keep up appearances, or our kids' activities that leave us feeling like chauffeurs, our possessions—including our time—can appear both insufficient and in jeopardy of evaporating before our eyes.

In light of this, we would do well to recall daily the prayer of Agur, recorded in Proverbs 30:8-9. This man wisely asked God for "neither poverty nor riches," a rather striking manner of requesting one's daily bread. For Agur looked into his own heart and realized that riches would cause him to have too much and disown God, saying "Who is the LORD?" But poverty would serve him no better, for his want would force him to "become poor and steal, and so dishonor the name of my God." Therefore, he asked God to give him only what he needed, no more and no less.

If we're honest with ourselves, we have to admit that we all suffer the effects of poverty and riches that Agur so astutely identified; sometimes we suffer them at virtually the same moment. We review our retirement accounts and in our pride forget that it's God who gives to us, yet in the next breath we fret that the market will tumble or—heaven forbid—we won't have enough to support our current lifestyle. We're arrogant and we're anxious, because we view ourselves as owners of our belongings rather than stewards of God's blessings.

Psalm 127 neatly sums up the serenity that stewardship brings. When a man embraces the truth that it's the Lord who builds and the Lord who guards, indeed, the Lord who owns, his labors are not painful, and his endeavors are not in vain. That man walks in the peace of knowing that God is the one who created heaven and earth and that man is simply a steward of that which has been entrusted to him. As a result, his sleep is sweet, and his desire is provided even while he rests.

We're presented daily with a choice: we can claim our "things" as our own and forget the Lord, who has provided them, or we can humbly manage the time, money, and relationships with which we've been entrusted. If we're spending too much time away from our families, chasing wealth and success, we need to revisit our priorities. Ultimately, the decision in this matter is a reflection of each man's view of himself. It's either a claim that we're our own gods or a recognition that we're not our own and "have been bought with a price" (1 Corinthians 6:20).

---

*Noel Bouché is the executive director of National Coalition for the Protection of Children & Families in Atlanta.*

# MAJESTY

JOE WHITE  ·····························································

*All the ends of the earth will remember and turn to the Lord, And all the families of the nations will worship before You. For the kingdom is the Lord's And He rules over the nations* (Psalm 22:27-28, NASB).

Cairo, where Christians even in recent years have been scoffed, mocked, and even martyred, probably isn't the place you would picture some of the sweetest, most intimate multinational worship ever offered up to the God of Isaac, Jacob, and His Son, Jesus Christ. But to my pleasure and surprise, it was one of the closest glimpses of heaven my eyes and ears have ever seen.

For several days I had the humble privilege of training 450 leaders from a dozen Middle Eastern and African nations in the shadow of the great Egyptian pyramids in a retreat and conference center just outside Cairo. From ages 17 to 65, these leaders from that area of the world gathered to praise, worship, and plan the pursuit of the Great Commission in their homelands.

The people's eyes were sparkling with the love of Christ. Many of them from the more hostile Islamic nations risk their lives and the security of their families to outwardly proclaim the name of Jesus and evangelize in His name.

My favorite part of the conference was the worship. The richness and majesty and awe that filled the conferees' hearts and filled the air were—well, they were heavenly.

The funny thing about it was, though, that I couldn't understand a word they sang, but I comprehended every note. Their music was pristine. Nothing but reverent worship came from their lips. My friends from remote nations around the globe experienced similar encounters. They sing because they love. They love because they live. They live because they sing.

Worship is as close to heaven as it gets this side of Jesus' return and the reunion of the saints. Worship is an encounter with God. It's a response to His love. Worship results in pressing yourself up to the divine mold of Christ. You *have* to walk away changed. If you don't walk away changed, you haven't encountered God.

My wife loves to dig into God's Word as the prospectors dug into the California mountains in the gold rush days. I love standing by her in church, because she sings with all her heart. But guess what—she's tone deaf. She can't carry a tune, can't even get close! She was even kicked out of sixth-grade choir and was dispatched to the library! But that doesn't deter her for a second. Debbie Jo doesn't sing to impress people—she sings to God.

Worship doesn't wait for perfect pitch, a beautiful sanctuary, or perfect people. All that's required is a sincere and humble heart, the welcoming of the work of Christ that leads you to the throne of grace, and the Spirit of the living God. You can close your eyes and enter any second, any minute, any hour, or any day. Take a moment in your travels to close your eyes and praise God today.

---

*Joe White is co-president and co-owner of Keanakuk Camps.*

# GOOD GRIEF

**KERRY WILLIS** ·····································································

*I will come back and take you to be with me that you also may be where I am* (John 14:3).

I was raised the oldest of the three sons of a commercial fisherman and his wife along the eastern seaboard of North Carolina. Specifically, home for me is a quaint North Carolina fishing island that borders the respected waters known as the Graveyard of the Atlantic. Today, all three of the fisherman's sons are preachers. I often say this about my own life: "I'm so grateful to be the son of a fisherman and a fisherman for the Son."

As a young island boy, I remember our dad leaving for days—sometimes weeks—at a time to provide for our family. It was hard for my mom, my brothers, and me to be apart from Daddy, but I never once doubted that he loved us. Each time he told us good-bye, tears lined his eyes. He often had to turn and exit in a hurry so we wouldn't see him crying. It was what love looked like to us.

Many years later, after I was grown, my dad and I were talking about personal regrets. Dad told me how guilty he felt because he missed so much of our daily lives. I quickly interrupted his misplaced guilt by saying, "Dad, knowing you wanted to be where we were was just as good as your being there."

It's true. You see, as humans we struggle with the God-only characteristic known as omnipresence. We cannot be all places simultaneously. However, when we grieve because we'll be apart from our loved ones, we're in fact giving one of the most undeniable forms of true love. It's called *good grief.*

In John 14—17, Jesus is preparing His disciples for His departure. These chapters are book-ended with the promise that our Lord desires *that we may be where He is.* His words in John 14:3 assure us, "I will come back and take you to be with me that you also may be where I am." John 17:24 also comforts our hearts as Jesus prays on behalf of us, His beloved ones, "Father, I want those you have given me to be with me where I am."

Amazingly, over the past year or so, when I've talked separately with my grown son and daughter about some of my regrets, they've said, "That's just false guilt, Dad." Yes, I've suffered severely with a lack of omnipresence in their lives, but I do know I've never wanted to be apart from them. One day, we'll never have to say good-bye again.

*Dearest Lord, help us to let our loved ones know that we truly want them to be where we are today and forever. As the time for your departure approached, you showed good grief to your loved ones. Help us to show good grief to our loved ones, too. In your name we pray. Amen.* 📖

---

*Kerry W. Willis is vision pastor of Harrisonburg First Church of the Nazarene, Harrisonburg, Virginia.*

# WOULD I BE LIKE JESUS?

STEVE GIRALI ········································

*He was despised and rejected by men, a man of sorrows, and familiar with suffering. Like one from whom men hide their faces he was despised, and we esteemed him not* (Isaiah 53:3).

Recently a friend of mine suffered a tragic heartache. Through a series of unjust events, his world began to crumble. A friend had betrayed him by making a power play that forced him out of his ministry. His nearly 30 years as a pastor came to a sudden end. A failing economy trapped him in a home he could no longer maintain or sell, which threatened to jeopardize his kid's college education. When life seemed darkest, it got worse when a dear friend and confidant suddenly passed away.

Broken and defeated, my friend cried out to God. God seemed so far away. The sense of abandonment was more than he could bear. He examined and reexamined his life to see if there was some sin that hindered his relationship with God. Day after day, he pleaded with God to make sense out of all the pain. But God was silent.

"Am I paying for my sin? Didn't Jesus really pay it *all*?" he asked. Before we could talk about that, he said, "And what about years of faithful ministry—is God putting me on the shelf?"

I didn't know how to answer. My friend was feeling betrayal, loss, grief, abandonment, condemnation, pain, and suffering. I hurt for him. If I could have taken away his suffering, I would have. It then dawned on me that Christ was being poured through me. My feelings were not so different than Jesus' feelings for my friend. So why didn't Jesus rescue him from the suffering? Why didn't He correct the injustice, heal the pain of searing loss, and restore the deep satisfaction of a fulfilled life again?

Have you ever prayed like this? *Christ, live through me; Lord Jesus, make me more like you; Father, help me to be more Christlike; Father, let me be conformed to the image of your risen Son.* When we pray those prayers, we expect to say profound things or feel God's power or demonstrate some wonderful attribute of God. We don't expect to be invited into His suffering.

We forget that Jesus was the Man of Sorrows. Isaiah says that he was "despised and rejected by men; a man of sorrows and acquainted with grief." Jeremiah depicts him as a suffering servant. During Jesus' ministry, we see him weep with compassion, experience ridicule and injustice, and know pain to the point of a cruel death. Conforming to Christ's image means that we'll know His suffering.

Is God walking you through a season of suffering? There may be some solace in knowing that Jesus has invited you to be more like Him. He also promises hope. He suffered so that we can be glorified with Him. He endured pain to free us from the bondage and consequence of sin. He really did pay it all. He was broken and bruised so that we could live life abundantly. The season of suffering will end. When it does, you'll know that Christ poured himself through you, He walked with you, He upheld you, and He will glorify you. 📖

---

*Steve Gerali is an author, consultant, professor, speaker, and mentor.*

# CHRISTIANITY BEGINS AT HOME

ROBERT BRIDGES ·············································

*Submit to one another out of reverence for Christ* (Ephesians 5:21).

When I was in seminary, my favorite devotional book was *Man to Man*, by Richard C. Halverson. This book had a lasting effect on me. I read it and made notes in it and in my Bible as I read.

In 1970 I read the selection titled "Christianity in the Home," based on Ephesians 5:21-64. Many have problems with this passage and want to discount its importance. Yet it's true. We're to love our wives as Christ loved the Church! We're to give ourselves to our spouses in the same way Jesus gave himself. This is *agape* love—self-sacrificing and all-giving. Would Jesus give less than His all for us, the Church? Of course not. We are to do the same in the establishment of our homes. That committed love begins with our spouses and flows to our children.

If you want to know the real nature of a man, check out his home, his spouse, his children.

William Barclay in his commentary on Ephesians says of this passage that husbands should love their wives in five ways—each as Christ loved the Church:

1. It must be as sacrificial love. He must love her not for her doing things for him but for his opportunity to do things for her.
2. It must be a purifying love. Real love is the great cleanser and purifier of all life.
3. It must be a caring love. A man must love his wife as he loves his own body. It is his duty to cherish her.
4. It is an unbreakable love. He would no more think of separating from her than he would think of tearing his own body apart.
5. The whole relationship is, as Paul puts it, *in the Lord.* In the Christian marriage there are not two partners but three—and the third is Christ.

Our marriages are the foundations of the homes. They mirror our character, and they establish the basis for our society.

But Paul goes on to how we treat our children. "Fathers, do not exasperate your children; instead, bring them up in the training and instruction of the Lord." Paul knew that a home built on the discipline and the admonition of the Lord would be a solid foundation and the cornerstone to a solid society.

Most of us would agree that our society is in turmoil. It has lost its footing and has strayed from the path of God's ways. The family is at risk. But true Christianity begins at home. During those times when we're away from our wives and children, we can reflect on our own leadership and commitment to them. We can pray that God will protect and strengthen them and make us more godly husbands and fathers. Solid homes built on solid biblical values are the foundation to a solid society. ▯

*Robert Bridges is executive vice president of Reformed Theological Seminary in Lexington, Kentucky.*

# THE GLORY OF GOD

RODDY BULLOCK ·····································

*One called out to another and said, "Holy, Holy, Holy, is the Lord of hosts, The whole earth is full of His glory"* (Isaiah 6:3, NASB).

Consider for a moment the glory of the Lord. We don't hear much about it today. Turn on the TV set, and you'll go through most channels with no mention of God's glory. In most workplaces you'll hear nothing of the glory of the Lord. In schools, including colleges and universities, the glory of the Lord has vanished. And unfortunately, even in the Church we hear little about the glory of the Lord.

One reason for this is that for years the primary expression of His glory, His creation, has been under relentless attack. Today many Christians have even bought into the idea that science has explained the creation of all living things as being the result of solely natural, purposeless processes. Believing that science is pure and its findings unassailable, many Christians have resigned themselves to weak or nonexistent beliefs in God's true, literal creation of life.

However, we minimize God's creation at the expense of His glory. Revelation 4:11 states, "You are worthy, our Lord and God, to receive glory and honor and power, for you created all things, and by your will they were created and have their being." And we're familiar with Psalm 19:1—"The heavens declare the glory of God; the skies proclaim the work of his hands." God's very handiwork praises Him and brings Him glory.

But who really believes this anymore? Unfortunately, many Christians tacitly agree with the director of the Vatican observatory who made news recently by expressing support of evolution as "a fundamental Church teaching," saying that believing in intelligent design "reduces and belittles God's power and might."

The apostle Paul describes such people in Romans 1:21-23: "Although they knew God, they neither glorified him as God nor gave thanks to him, but their thinking became futile and their foolish hearts were darkened. Although they claimed to be wise, they became fools and exchanged the glory of the immortal God for images made to look like mortal man and birds and animals and reptiles."

We must approach the truth claims of science carefully, because God's truth is not changed by the false declarations of the world's wise. And when we contemplate creation, we consider much more than an academic question—we touch on the very glory of the Lord. ▮▮▮

---

*Roddy Bullock is senior counsel in the intellectual property division of Procter & Gamble Company.*

# ACCEPTING RESPONSIBILITY

JEFF BYERS ·································································

*Then David said to Nathan, "I have sinned against the Lord." Nathan replied, "The Lord has taken away your sin. You are not going to die"* (2 Samuel 12:13).

How many times when I've been on the road have I rationalized or justified my actions? "You deserve it, you want it, you need it" are the enemy's encouragement in the midst of a spiritual battle. It's during these times we can stand on God's promise in 1 Corinthians 10:13: "No temptation has seized you except that which is common to man. And God is faithful; he will not let you be tempted beyond what you can bear. But when you are tempted, he will also provide a way out so you can stand up under it."

It should provide great comfort knowing that no matter what the situation we face, God will provide a way out. Unfortunately, if we're not under the continual power of the Holy Spirit, we find our flesh still takes over at times as it did for David, and we never know how far into sin it may lead us. In David's case it led to adultery, lying, and murder. When confronted by Nathan, he owned up to it. God wants a contrite and repentant heart.

I'm a man who grew up without a real relationship with Jesus. My father passed away when I was 10 years old, and my mom did a great job trying to keep us plugged into church. However, it didn't lead me to much spiritual growth. That didn't start happening until my mid- to late-30s. By this time I had developed some behaviors that were controlling me and not pleasing to God.

I've found that I'm not alone—whether it be Internet addiction, television, video game addiction, pornography, gambling, drinking, strip clubs, drugs, anger, or whatever, many guys have kept these things hidden. They're hidden from wives, friends, and church, even our men's group.

I've found that freedom from the hidden darkness comes when we accept responsibility by confessing our sins to God and to one another, as James 5:16 instructs: "Confess your sins to each other and pray for each other that you may be healed. The prayer of a righteous man is powerful and effective."

I was faced with confessing a gambling addiction to a very close friend of mine several years ago. Returning from a Gamblers Anonymous meeting one Wednesday evening, I received a call from Jon, who asked, "What's up?" At that moment, driving down the freeway, I faced that moment of decision—lie or tell the truth. The Lord said, "Trust him." Even though I was ashamed and worried about what Jon would think of me, I told him. I confessed to another brother the struggles I had been having, and immediately the weight of the hidden sin was lifted.

Have you been hiding something? Is there darkness in some area of your life? Pray that God will deliver you, and find a trusted friend in which you can confide.  📖

---

*Jeff Byers is senior marketing director of Financial Services.*

# AS CHRIST LOVED THE CHURCH

NOEL BOUCHÉ ·····················································

*I saw heaven opened, and behold, a white horse, and He who sat on it is called Faithful and True* (Revelation 19:11, NASB).

It is written that we are to love our wives "just as Christ loved the church and gave himself up for her" (Ephesians 5:25). We read this verse and meditate on it at just about every wedding we attend. Yet this eloquent description of the archetypal marriage begs the question "What does it mean to give myself up for my wife?" While we must follow Christ's example and be ready to face death literally for our loved ones, most of us will not be confronted with the decision to die a substitutionary death for our wives. But physical death was not the only way Jesus gave himself up.

In the Revelation, John saw the bridegroom returning, and He was called according to two primary attributes—faithfulness and truth. Imagine this! John is gazing upon the "Mighty God" and the "Prince of Peace" (Isaiah 9:6), the One to whom all praise is due, and yet the name He chooses to go by reflects His attachment and commitment to us, whose frames are "but dust" (Psalm 103:14). I must ask myself if I'm defining myself in the same manner as my Lord—as a faithful and true bridegroom—or am I defining myself primarily by my professional title, by my accomplishments, or by my net worth? Am I "my beloved's"—or am I mine?

It is in this way that we can give ourselves up and "die daily" (1 Corinthians 15:31), thus loving our wives as Christ loved the Church. When we are "faithful and true," we put our wives first, ourselves second. We value their hope and confidence in our fidelity—both on the road and when we are at home—above our own wants and desires. Each of us is "exhilarated always with her love" and infatuated with her body "at all times" (Proverbs 5:19).

It must be emphasized, though, that our "death" cannot be contingent on our wives' reciprocation. Jesus was faithful and true to the point of crucifixion not only if we loved Him in the same way; indeed, it was because we had not loved Him that His death was necessary.

It's the same in our case. We must "give ourselves up" precisely because our wives, like us, are imperfect and will at times cause us hurt. It's only in this way that we're truly "crucified with Christ" (Galatians 2:20).

Each day we must decide to be faithful and true husbands. The world conspires against this, because being faithful is the very reflection of God's love for humanity. But when we daily choose to be filled with God's Spirit, we allow ourselves to be conformed to His image, His faithfulness, and His truth. We can then sing over our wives as He sings over his people: "I will betroth you to me in righteousness and in justice, in lovingkindness and in compassion, and I will betroth you to me in faithfulness" (Hosea 2:19-20, NASB). 📖

---

*Noel Bouché is executive director of National Coalition for the Protection of Children & Families in Cincinnati.*

# AM I A SLAVE?

GORDON DOUGHMAN ·······························

*The rich rule over the poor, and the borrower is servant to the lender* (Proverbs 22:7).

The United States is drowning in a sea of debt. The national debt stands at 9.6 *trillion* dollars! That's about $31,650 dollars for every man, woman, and child in the country. The average household owes approximately $18,650 in consumer debt, not including a mortgage, with about $8,000 of that debt on high-interest credit cards. Because of this, many families earning a good income are living paycheck-to-paycheck, barely able to make ends meet. The statistics are very sobering, and surveys have shown that Christian families are not all that different from non-Christian families.

While the Bible does not prohibit the use of debt, it does contain numerous warnings and admonitions regarding it. Debt should be used with caution for the following reasons. First, debt presumes upon the future. When we use debt to finance purchases, we make the assumption that our income will remain steady or that we will not have any unexpected expenses in the future. This is almost never the case. As Proverbs 27:1 warns, "Do not boast about tomorrow, for you do not know what a day may bring forth."

Second, debt tends to obscure the true cost of items purchased. For example, the purchase of a $1,000 item using a credit card charging 19-percent interest will require approximately eight years to pay back and cost nearly $1,000 in interest if only minimum monthly payments are made. Thus, the $1,000 item really ends up costing double its original purchase price. In addition, this does not count the lost interest that could be earned if the monthly interest payments sent to the credit card company were invested. That could easily add another $500 to $700 to the cost of the item. Paying more than necessary for an item is not being a good steward of the resources with which God has blessed us.

Third, debt can delay God's plan for our lives. God promised that He will provide for our needs—not all our wants. If we're indebted to creditors, it may delay God's calling on our lives to a profession or even a full-time ministry position that may pay less than what's required to meet our debts.

Finally, to live faithfully as a Christian, we're called to live a life of delayed gratification, denying ourselves the sinful pleasures of this world as we set our sights on eternity with Christ. This principle can also be applied to our finances. Rather than using debt, which allows us to experience instant gratification for the things we want, we should work and save for those things that we believe will bring honor to God and His Son.

"Let no debt remain outstanding, except the continuing debt to love one another" (Romans 13:8).

---

*Gordon Doughman is an elder in the Evangelical Community Church in Cincinnati, Ohio.*

# THE CHARACTER OF A GODLY MAN
## (PART ONE)

STEVE GERALI ····················································

*A new command I give you: Love one another. As I have loved you, so you must love one another* (John 13:34).

For years I've had the privilege of mentoring late-adolescent young men in their journey of becoming God-honoring men. I've watched these guys leave childish ways and become men of great character who have taken their rightful places as godly fathers, churchmen, and community leaders. The journey is never easy, but it always begins with a simple question: "When life comes to a close, what do you want people to say about you?"

Most late adolescents have difficulty deciding what their college major will be, let alone pondering an end-of-life question. Immediately they respond by saying things like being a good father, making a difference, and impacting the workplace. But the majority of the time they say, "I hope people say I was a godly man."

Most adult men when faced with the same question may have a difficult time answering. If the man is a Christian, he's likely to give this same answer. It can be a true and noble answer, and it can also be a typical churchy clichéd answer. When I hear a guy answer in such a way, I applaud it, but then I ask a follow-up question: "What does a godly man look like?"

That's the stumper! Many men can't wrap their minds around that one. If they answer, it's usually with another churchy response that takes them down the road to an unattainable, impractical, theologically rhetorical response. Over the years I've struggled with this same question in my own life. In wrestling through those questions with these great men, I've come to some simple and yet profound conclusions.

There is one outstanding characteristic of a God-honoring man. If at the end of life people can't boldly ascribe this characteristic to you, then they can't say that you were a godly man. It's *love*. Jesus was asked what the greatest commandment was, and He said "to *love* God and *love* others." We call it the Great Commandment. Later Jesus reiterated this by leaving His "new command" to His disciples (John 13:34). As matter of fact, Jesus said that people "will know that you are my disciples by your *love* for one another" (John 13:35). It's a defining mark. Men don't usually want such a "feminine" attribute to be the defining mark of their life. We need to see that this is a godly attribute. If *love* isn't among the first characteristics that people think of when reflecting on you, then they can't say that you're a Christian, let alone a godly man.

Do the people who regularly come into contact with you know that you're marked by love? Would your colleagues say that you're a loving man—not just a loving father, husband, or son? How do they experience that love?

---

*Steve Girali is an author, consultant, professor, speaker, and mentor.*

# THE CHARACTER OF A GODLY MAN
(PART TWO)

STEVE GERALI ·····················································

*He has showed you, O man, what is good. And what does the LORD require of you? To act justly and to love mercy and to walk humbly with your God* (Micah 6:8).


Jason, an engaging, electric 20-year-old, sat across the table from me as we ate lunch. "Doc, I believe that if a man is God-honoring, then he's kind of like a modern-day warrior who stands up for the truth—that's how I want to be known," he proclaimed.

I agreed with Jason that there is an archetype of a warrior in the landscape of a godly man's roles, but it doesn't look as if Jason, or many other Christian men, described it. The prophet Micah described this warrior not as a champion of truth or right-ness but one who is *good*.

Jesus says that men will "see your good deeds and praise your Father in heaven" (Matthew 5:16). Jesus modeled this throughout His ministry. He went about doing *good*. Goodness is the salt and light that Jesus speaks of. Paul also says that we're God's workmanship created in Christ Jesus for *good* works" (Ephesians 2:10). Countless more times Paul and Peter pepper their letters with admonition to live *good*, evidenced by good works. Paul even reminds us that *goodness* is among the fruit that the Holy Spirit produces in our lives (Galatians 5:22). *Goodness* becomes a defining mark in a godly man. *Goodness* should permeate all that he is and does.

This good warrior doesn't use a sword, and he isn't brazen to proclaim his idea of truth. Instead, he acts justly and loves being merciful. Instead of standing boldly, looking for a battle to fight, he walks humbly with God. This is a *good* man.

Jason looked at me and said, "You mean if people are going to know you as a godly man, they need to say you're a *good guy*?" The way he said it was like fingernails being scratched across a blackboard.

"Yep, if goodness isn't among the first words ascribed to you, then people will have a hard time saying you were God-honoring," I responded.

"But good guys finish last and girls don't date *good* guys. That's like saying we're just brothers and sisters in Christ. If you're a *good guy* then girls just see you as a brother," Jason added.

Jason hit the nail on the head—being a good guy isn't tough or manly. Every message that guys receive about masculinity is powerful, and *goodness* isn't in that arsenal. This makes it even more difficult to be a *good* man. We've been wired up to shun the *good guy* label. The only way we can correct the trajectory is to rely humbly on Christ.

Jason put down his sword that day. He started a journey of goodness. He realized that the only way that good works could come from him was if his character was defined by goodness. He became a good warrior who humbly strolled through life with his God. When people saw Jason's good works, they saw His God.

Do people say that you're a good man? Can you identify ways that goodness is consistently played out in your life? Do the choices you make in public and in private reflect your desire to please God?

---

*Steve Girali is an author, consultant, professor, speaker, and mentor.*

# PICKING APPLES AND PEACHES

JOHN LEWIS ⸳⸳⸳⸳⸳⸳⸳⸳⸳⸳⸳⸳⸳⸳⸳⸳⸳⸳⸳⸳⸳⸳⸳⸳⸳⸳⸳⸳⸳⸳⸳⸳⸳⸳⸳⸳⸳⸳⸳⸳⸳⸳⸳⸳⸳⸳⸳⸳⸳⸳⸳⸳⸳⸳⸳⸳⸳⸳⸳⸳⸳

Suppose that by some supernatural means you were able to remember each of the important things you accomplished in life. Suppose, too, that you knew you would die in the next several seconds. Suppose someone then asked you, "What was the most important thing you accomplished in life?"

What would you say? Would it be that you consistently achieved one million dollars annual sales of some group of products, insurance programs, or real estate over several consecutive years? Would it be that you did an outstanding job in leading an important company, hospital, or labor union as chairman, CEO, or business manager? Perhaps you think of your dedicated service as principal, pastor, doctor, or repairman. Or maybe it's your multiple inventions or discoveries in computers, plant genetics, or robotics.

How about your family? Where do your wife and children fit in your list? Do they love and respect you? Do they see you as an example of a godly husband and father? Do they look to you as the spiritual leader of their family? Are they walking with the Lord as you've taught them in the life you modeled for them? Would they point to you as an example of a man whom others should emulate because of your godly character and lifestyle? Will they desire to raise and train their children as you raised them?

The most important thing I've accomplished is modeling my life on Jesus as much as humanly possible. What does that look like? That means I show and tell my wife and children I love them as often as I can. I traveled outside the United States three to four months each year during my 32-year business career. The last thing I said when I left was the simple phase "I love you!" Even today I still say it to them often. I tried to love them as God's creatures, as the people God brought into my life, as unconditionally as I could. They, too, have been renewed by His grace. They, too, sometimes do and say things that require me to forgive them, as God has forgiven me. I consciously chose to live before their watching eyes, setting an example for them to follow, whether in loving, forgiving, working, playing or just hanging out.

That also means I consciously made choices to be with them. Rather than going golfing or quail hunting on weekends, or simply going to my workbench in the basement to be alone, I intentionally asked them what they would like to do and then went about doing it as quickly as I could. Jesus says He loves us. How do you define love? My definition of love is *selflessness.* Can you think of anything Jesus didn't deserve? Anything He couldn't have asked for?

What did He do? He was totally selfless! He gave Himself to reconcile filthy, fallen man to his righteous and holy Father. He sacrificed himself, His glory, and His honor for someone other than himself.

What's your definition of love? How do your children know you love them? Because you say so, or because you *do* so?

Our three kids told us some years ago that they wanted to pick apples. After picking, we worked in our kitchen as a family to make applesauce. We encouraged our children to invite their friends. During our car ride, we discussed things that concerned them and tried to answer their questions. Then we asked questions such as why God made the universe, why there's absolute truth, who their friends were, and what they were doing. No, I'm not a scratch golfer, nor do I serve as chair of a country club membership committee, but my wife and I have raised what we think are three pretty neat daughters. And we're still picking apples with our seven grandchildren.

Giving yourself to your wife and children also means spending time talking about Jesus, praying and memorizing scripture with them in the morning and in the evenings on every day of the week—all the time. Do your wife, kids, and grandkids know that Jesus means more to you than anything else? Have they watched you endure hardship and tough places when you drew strength from the sovereign God of the universe? Have you taken time to explain to them from time to time why that's the way you choose to live and make your decisions? Or are you so involved in doing things at church, the office, the club, that they don't have enough time to be with you to really know who you are?

Jesus demonstrated His love for the Church, according to Ephesians 5:25, by giving himself away. It was His number-one priority. Can you or I do any less? We'll be blessed for it! ▮▮▮

---

*John B. Lewis is an adjunct professor at Missouri Baptist University in St. Louis.*

# LOVE THE LORD WITH ALL YOUR STRENGTH

JACK SCHRAND ·····························································

*Love the Lord your God with all your heart and with all your soul and with all your strength and with all your mind; and love your neighbor as yourself* (Luke 10:27).

It takes a man of strength to pull off the command of Luke 10:27. He must be a man with strength of character and strength of conviction. Why? Because it takes more than what he has within him. It tears against the grain for us to accomplish this. It's not what we want to do. For this to happen, we have to murder our flesh, our personal wants. Therefore, we must *surrender* to God and ask Him to make this happen in us. Once the Lord accomplishes this in us, it's a comfortable place to be. But the road there is not. God must first build His strength and character in us for this to be possible.

What will this even look like? Is there a model or template for us to use to get a glimpse of what this will be? Yes, there is. First look at Jesus. He lived it as our example. He loved His Father and His Bride (the Church) this way. He also gave us a list of practical steps or benchmarks for us to follow in 1 Corinthians 13:4-7. We typically think of these verses more as they relate to one another. And while they do, may I suggest that they first apply to our relationship with God?

Paul starts out by encouraging us to be patient with God. This isn't easy. We want instant results; but those seldom last. God wants to build character and perseverance in us. That's a process that simply takes time. We learn from mistakes and hurts. We learn to trust God when we can't see the end. This is hard for me. Perhaps it is for you too.

Next, the Lord wants to develop kindness in us and strip away envy. Yet envy and unkindness are our defense mechanisms. We use these to get our way at God's expense. We show it often toward other people. We even feel justified. God refers to this as self-righteousness, which He abhors. When I'm not on my guard, I often fall into envy and unkindness. How about you? This is where I must simply get to the point at which I say, *Jesus, please take over!* I think of Peter, who cried out, "Lord, help me. I'm drowning!"

The next few are very similar attacks on my natural desires. "Love does not boast; it is not proud. It is not rude and is not self-seeking." Each of these are ways I try to build myself up at someone else's expense. Like most sin, it feels good for the moment. But these cut a person to the core and tear at God's heart. Sometimes these are my responses when others treat me in these ways. *God, do you know what they said about me?* He answers, *Yes. And do you remember what you did to me? I still forgave you and welcomed you.*

Then Paul quickly shares the next few steps. Love is not easily angered and keeps no record of wrongs. It does not delight in evil but seeks and delights in finding out the truth. When our heart is filled with anger, it naturally ignores the truth. Have you ever been angry with God? It's that self-protection thing again. It's one of Satan's dirty little tricks. God's example to us showed us the importance of forgetting our wrongs and flooded us with forgiveness. As difficult as forgiveness often is, we must do the same. Christ will enable us to do it if we truly seek His help.

As we allow Christ to help us with this forgiveness, the remaining steps are a natural outgrowth. We see them in God's attitude toward us. He always protects us and trusts us. He gives us hope and perseveres through our failings and setbacks. Do we deserve it? Definitely not! He does these things anyway. You see, God's love *never* fails. He looks beyond the moment into what we'll become. He trusts himself with our future.

As we learn how to love God in this way, He'll guarantee our success. Then, by God's strength, let Him show you how to love your neighbor as yourself. It won't be easy. But you must be the man, God's man, and be strong. If you're married, God says to love your wife as Christ loved His church. He didn't say, "If you want to." He said, "Just do it." He also guarantees our success if we surrender to Christ in us. 📖

---

*Jack Schrand is a real estate salesman with Coldwell Banker West Shell: The Schrand Team in Cincinnati, Ohio.*

# PRIDE

DAN REXROTH ·····················································

What is the first step to ruining your life? Of all the character traits, which is the one you must guard your heart against most? What is the vice that can lead to all sorts of sin?

We notice this trait in others but rarely in ourselves. Yet every one of us can be found guilty of it at times. What is this awful thing? *Pride.*

No fault can lead to more sin than pride. When we think we're invincible, we fail. When we think we're above temptation, we fall. When we think we're popular, clever, or better than others, we alienate.

Pride is the pleasure of thinking we're better than others. Having a little more money, intelligence, or being better in any way is the goal of pride. The feeling of superiority and power is what pride is all about.

Why is pride dangerous? It's the most deadly of sins, because it leads to all manner of other sins. Pride comes before every fall. It swells with invincibility and independence. It has been the chief cause of misery, regret, and grief in every family since the days of Adam and Eve. Pride causes us to lose a right perspective on our life, attitudes, and behaviors.

The truth is that none of us can resist temptation and avoid a fall without the help of God and the support of those closest to us. We must daily declare our dependence on Him and place ourselves under the authority of others.

The cure to pride is forgetting about yourself. It was once said, "We should not think less of ourselves—but rather think of ourselves less." Focusing on God's greatness makes us recognize our own shortcomings. Focusing on others diminishes our own selfish desires. Recognize that you need God and others for your very survival—because you do.

Pride and independence seem to be the way of the world. And even though the world is crowded with people, isolation and anonymity are common. The combination of these is a recipe for disaster in your Christian walk. Resisting temptations can never be accomplished through our own strength. Our strength comes through total dependence on Christ and support from fellow Christians. With humility and dependence comes wisdom.

Samuel Butler said, "The truest characters of ignorance are vanity, pride, and arrogance." Recognize your tendency toward pride, and consciously place yourself under the authority of God and others. It will save your life.

*Dan Rexroth is president and CEO of Premier Life/John Knox Village, Lenexa, Kansas.*

# WHEN THE BATTLE GETS PERSONAL
## (PART ONE)

TED ROBERTS ·······································································

*Each one is tempted when, by his own evil desire, he is dragged away and enticed. Then, after desire has conceived, it gives birth to sin; and sin, when it is full-grown, gives birth to death* (James 1:14-15).

I was a new Marine Corps fighter pilot. When you haven't seen combat, they call you a "nugget." But God was about to place some real Kingdom gold into my soul. I was enticed to fly into what is called a "flack trap" in Vietnam—a target set up to look tempting but is designed by the enemy to shoot you down.

That moment flashed back into my mind once I realized I was struggling with bondage to sexual issues. The battle became personal, just as it had over the skies of southeast Asia. Since that realization, I have counseled others who have faced sexual bondage. By bondage I mean that they've continued to repeat a behavior that they know is harmful in spite of the negative consequences.

- Sixty-six percent of Internet-using men between the ages of 18 and 34 look at online pornography at least once a month.
- Thirty-three percent of pastors state they have visited a sexually explicit web site. Some recent surveys put the number much higher—into the 50-percent range.
- The largest consumer of Internet pornography is the 12- to 17-year-old age group. This means that we're in for a tsunami of bondage in the next generation of leaders.

You are at war, and you are not the only one fighting the battle. How can we get out of the bondage and help others? Well, I gained some real wisdom from that flack trap years ago.

**Realize that it's not going to get better simply by your trying harder.** The enemy had me in his sights, and no matter how hard I twisted and turned, it wasn't going to get any better. The level of sexual stimulation in our culture today can create a deep bondage. James 1:14-15 points out the ruthlessness of your spiritual enemy. And when it comes to sexual issues I have literally lost count of the number of leaders and men who have said to me, "Ted, I have prayed, fasted, read my Bible, repented, got in a group, and told God I will never do it again a thousand times, *but it doesn't work.*"

**Don't play the look-good game.** Forget about looking good! Your soul is on the line if you let this thing keep chewing you up in secret. We're talking about losing your marriage, your family, your integrity! Get some help—*now.* As the huge tracers went flying by my canopy, I cried out for help. I didn't say to myself, *I don't want to appear as if I can't handle this.* I needed help, and I admitted it and cried out to someone who knew how to deal with the problem.

Freedom is possible when we cry out to God and others. That doesn't end the battle. Tomorrow we will look at two other steps.  📖

---

*Ted Roberts is with Pure Desire Ministries, East Hill Church, Gresham, Oregon.*

# WHEN THE BATTLE GETS PERSONAL
## (PART TWO)

TED ROBERTS ·····················································

*So those whom God set apart, he called; and those he called, he put right with himself, and he shared his glory with them* (Romans 8:30, TEV).

I can still vividly remember the golf-ball-sized tracer rounds zipping past the canopy as I violently jerked my fighter aircraft through the sky. I was fighting for my life. But I was trapped, and time was running out. As I mentioned yesterday, things started turning around for me when I realized that trying harder wasn't working and I cried out for help.

That lesson I learned in combat also saved my life in my battle for sexual purity. I've discovered that despite the shame that would tell me to hide and pretend that I had it together, real freedom is found only in honesty, because you're only as sick as your secrets. Purity is never possible without partnership. Every road warrior *must* be part of a combat team in our sex-soaked society. And we must understand two other critical truths.

**1. We must understand the tactics of the enemy we're fighting.** I cried out to my flight leader, who was an experienced combat pilot. He immediately realized the trouble I was in. He also understood where the enemy would position their weapons, and he unloaded on them. He saved my life. Sexual bondages and addictions are one of the master strategies of hell. They promise you everything and give you nothing. Both the Old and New Testament are replete with examples of this master strategy that hell has used so effectively through the ages. To get free, you have to do more than get into an accountability group. You also need to find a group of men who can help you discover the resources that you need in order to walk into real freedom, not just a bunch of guys to whom you promise to try harder after you relapse.

**2. Get a renewed grip on your God-given vision.** This battle is not about how bad you are. The battle is about the fact that God has called you and set you apart in Christ. For years hell has been telling you that you're worthless. For most men, the struggles with sexual sin started in their early teens. This battle is about the call of God on your life. Rise up, my friend, and realize that this is not just about you but about all the other men you'll be able to help. If you face this battle and win, by the grace of God their lives can be changed. That mission years ago was to keep our troops on the ground alive, and because I was able to win the battle, they lived. The statistics are clear—the majority of men sitting in church today are losing the battle for sexual purity. They need you to win. Come join us in this battle. Let's hurt hell for a change! 📖

---

*Ted Roberts is with Pure Desire Ministries, East Hill Church, Gresham, Oregon.*

# MEDITATE ON THESE THINGS

GENE DEMENT ·······················································

*Whatever things are true, whatever things are noble, whatever things are just, whatever things are pure, whatever things are lovely, whatever things are of good report, if there is any virtue and if there is anything praiseworthy—meditate on these things* (Philippians 4:8, NKJV).

One of the most important things I've learned since becoming a Christian is the value of putting good things into my mind and heart so that my thoughts are pure and my actions deliberate. That is why my Bible devotions and prayer life are so critical to my successful spiritual walk.

Seldom do we stop to think about the process by which our thoughts control our activities. Our conscious minds are what we have control of, and the mental images we create allow us to plan our daily activities. The subconscious, however, is more fluid and difficult to understand. Most of us feel we understand pretty well how the conscious mind works. Consciousness is being aware of our thinking, feeling, and actions. We control these thoughts and actions.

The subconscious is not under our direct control, and these thoughts are in the mind beyond our conscious awareness. We've all had the experience of saying or doing something that we had not really thought about at the time. For instance, have you ever tried to solve a problem for which the answer just wouldn't come? And then later, when you weren't really thinking about it, the answer just popped into your mind. For this reason it's extremely important that we think positive thoughts about our spouse and family. When we travel, we can carry a photo of them and view it often, thinking how beautiful they are. Then giving good compliments when we return comes much easier and with more meaning. If, on the other hand, we're feeding our minds with lustful thoughts or pornography, it will be hard to think good thoughts about our spouses and family and consequently difficult to give them compliments and reassurance.

The point is to empty your subconscious mind of bad thoughts and fill it with good thoughts. Since the subconscious is the sum of all your past and current experiences, it makes sense to fill it with as much good as possible. In that manner, good thoughts and actions will be the product of your behavior.

"Your word have I hidden in my heart, that I might not sin against You" (Psalm 119:11, NKJV).  📖

---

*Gene Dement is a physician in Neosho, Missouri.*

# DO YOU REMEMBER?

CHUCK STECKER ·····················································

*They forgot what he had done, the wonders he had shown them* (Psalm 78:11).

If you want to look at one of the most incredible reoccurring themes in the Bible, it's the issue of men of God forgetting all that God had done for them.

As men, we have this incredible propensity of living for the moment. Yesterday is long gone, and tomorrow is out there somewhere. What really counts is today. The problem with that mentality is that we miss much of the strength that God has intended for us.

We should draw strength from remembering all that God has done for us. As if salvation was not enough, there's always so much more for which to be grateful.

God uses the majority of Psalm 78 to remind the Israelites of all He had done. It also emphasizes that after all of the incredible wonders He had shown them, they continued to turn their backs on Him.

Today most Christian guys live in a what-have-you-done-for-me-lately world, often forgetting that God has a long history of loving us more than we can begin to love Him back.

Not only is it important for us to remember all that God has done for us, but it's also critical that we pass on that history of God's love to our children and our children's children.

When we begin to recall God's faithfulness, it's important that we focus not only on the really big blessings but also on even the smallest of blessings. Equally important is that we remember that God has done all these things out of His incredible love for us.

My grandchildren love me to tell them stories of God's love and faithfulness in our lives, because it also speaks of His love for *them*. When God blesses our family, He blesses all of us. They draw strength from a history of blessings.

We tell the stories to remind them of the past so that they can draw strength and know that they can trust God in the future in their own lives.

As you have quiet moments on the road, spend some time thinking about what God has done for you. Write those things down, and share them with your family.

If you don't remember, how will they? 📖

---

*Chuck Stecker is founder and president of A Chosen Generation, Littleton, Colorado.*

# WHERE DO YOU RANK ON THE WORLD'S "RICH LIST"?

**DICK TOWNER** ····················································

*Command those who are rich in this present world not to be arrogant nor to put their hope in wealth, which is so uncertain, but to put their hope in God, who richly provides us with everything for our enjoyment. Command them to do good, to be rich in good deeds, and to be generous and willing to share* (1 Timothy 6:17-18).

There's a lot to reflect upon in just the two verses from Paul's words to Timothy in 1 Timothy 6:17-18. Read the verses slowly, and underline what jumps out at you; then ask God why those words were the ones His Holy Spirit brought to your attention.

Perhaps you felt the words didn't speak directly to you since they were for those who are rich in this world. But the Web site <www.globalrichlist.com> indicates that $50,000 in annual income puts you in that category. Annual income of $40,000 is in the top 3 percent. Take a moment to reflect on your status in the world rich list.

As a final point to ponder, note that the statement that God has provided us with all things to enjoy is immediately followed by another command—to do good and be rich in good works and to be generous. Those of the prosperity gospel persuasion might stop with the statement that all things are for our enjoyment. An interpretation that is more in keeping with Jesus' teaching would be that if we've received more than what we need for ourselves and those dependent upon us, it's not for increasing our standard of living but for increasing our standard of *giving* and *sharing*.

It may just be that the maximum enjoyment we can receive from that which has been entrusted to us is that which comes from sharing and giving it away.

How can you do good, be rich in good works, and be generous today?

---

*Dick Towner is executive director of Good $ense Stewardship Movement, Elgin, Illinois.*

# OUR THOUGHTS

MARK LINGLE ·····························································

*Fix your thoughts on what is true and good and right. Think about things that are pure and lovely, and dwell on the fine, good things in others. Think about all you can praise God for and be glad about. Keep putting into practice all you learned from me and saw me doing, and the God of peace will be with you* (Philippians 4:8-9, TLB).

Are we living what Paul writes here in Philippians? Are we contemplating the good in others or even in ourselves? It seems that as men, we tend not to think about what is pure, lovely, good, and right simply because we're human and we fall into what is easy and natural. We all know practice is hard work and that putting things that are pure, lovely, good and right into our everyday lives requires effort—requires work. Skills like riding a bicycle, shaving, or simply pushing the button on the remote to lower the garage door become automatic skills—skills that, after we've done them over and over a number of times, we do without even thinking about them. Like anything else we do in life, if we practice, it becomes natural.

Let our thoughts become natural, incorporating pure thoughts, lovely gestures, good attributes, and right decisions, whether in our relationships with others or even in our relationship with God. In our alone times, these good habits can bring us strength. Where are your thoughts right now? Do they need some adjustments? 📖

---

*Mark Lingle is director of World Sport Stacking Association, Littleton, Colorado.*

# FOR BETTER OR WORSE

AL COLE ···················································································

*Let thy fountain be blessed: and rejoice with the wife of thy youth. Let her be as the loving hind and pleasant roe; let her breasts satisfy thee at all times; and be thou ravished always with her love* (Proverbs 5:18-19, KJV).

There are two ways to become an expert on marriage. One is to read every book on marriage you can get your hands on. I took the other path: I became an expert on marriage by making every conceivable mistake a husband could make.

Mark Twain observed, "No man or woman really knows what perfect love is until they have been married a quarter of a century." I've been married for 28 years, and I'm still learning. A lot is written about special date nights, doing chores around the house, and other ideas to spice up your marriage. Those are good, but experience has taught me that just as the Lord wants us to *be* with Him rather than *do* for Him, our wives desire us to be emotionally connected with them.

Here's a simple prayer my wife and I put together to help remind us what a godly marriage is supposed to be. Perhaps as you travel you can begin to craft a similar prayer with your spouse.

*Dear Lord, we renew our commitment today to live as husband and wife, as you intended, until death separates us (Matthew 19:6). We promise to demonstrate our love for each other daily in both word and deed (1 Corinthians 13:4), and to live in obedience to your will for our lives (Ephesians 5:22, 25).*

*As we die to ourselves this day (Philippians 2:3), we promise we will endure all hardships and respect and honor one another as the unique individuals you created us to be (Romans 12:9). We ask that you strengthen the bonds of trust between us, removing doubts that might threaten our serenity (Job 31:6).*

*As we go through our day, fill us with a spirit of optimism based on the promises of Jesus (John 10:10). As you have commanded, we will encourage each other to grow in our knowledge of you and use the spiritual gifts you have given us (Hebrews 3:13), savoring the uniqueness that we each bring to this marriage (Song of Solomon 7:6).*

*Teach us to be tenderhearted and forgiving when one of us stumbles (Ephesians 4:32) so that we may live in unity of spirit and enjoy peace and harmony in our home (Romans 15:5). Let our hearts be as open books, concealing nothing from each other (Samuel 22:25), and may we be ever thankful for your lovingkindness, which begins fresh every morning (Psalm 89:1).*

*Enable us to set aside our prideful nature and walk humbly, hand in hand, toward the throne of grace (1 Peter 5:6). We ask you to rekindle our passion, so that we might delight in each other (Proverbs 5:18-19). We vow today that, with your help, we will seek to live righteous lives that will bring honor to your name. In Christ Jesus. Amen.*

*Al Cole is executive director of National Coalition for the Protection of Children & Families in Atlanta.*

# CHOICE AND CONSEQUENCE

CHARLES DAVIS ·····················································

*Choose for yourselves this day whom you will serve, whether the gods your forefathers served beyond the river, or the gods of the Amorites, in whose land you are living. But as for me and my household, we will serve the Lord* (Joshua 24:15).

In a very real sense, life is but a series of choices, and success is related to our ability to make the right choices. Some of our choices are major and life-changing: who we marry, what we choose to do for a living, where we choose to live. On the other hand, most of our choices are not so significant. However, when we look at the choices we make, we find certain truths apply to all of them.

First, every choice has a consequence. This is obvious with the major choices of life, but it's equally true for even the most minor decisions we make. Routine decisions become habits. And our habits develop into our lifestyle, which then determines our character.

Character is described as the choices we make when no one is looking. Thus, even the insignificant choices have consequences, because they influence our lifestyle and character. These daily choices directly impact us when we make major decisions.

Second, we're individually responsible for every choice we make. Our self-centered society would tell us that we can and should avoid responsibility for any choice that has a negative consequence. However, when we're honest with ourselves, we realize that we're responsible for the decisions we make—big and small.

These same truths apply to the choices we make in our spiritual pilgrimage. Many choices we make seem minor or insignificant—daily devotions, prayer at meals, regular church attendance. However, they have significant consequences. The choices we make to grow spiritually become not only habits but also the very fiber of our lifestyle and the essence of our character. When we face a major challenge—a crisis in our health, a troubled relationship, a major temptation—we're greatly strengthened in choosing our response if we've made the seemingly routine choice to grow daily in His Word and His Grace.

Choosing to serve God does not stop with the initial major choice but rather continues with a series of daily choices—some minor and routine, others major and significant in their consequences. But it's the daily choices that strengthen us. So choose daily whom you'll serve. As for me and my house, we will serve the Lord.

---

*Charles Davis is an appeals court judge for the State of Florida.*

# YOU REALLY DO MATTER

H. B. LONDON ····························································

Before I became "pastor to pastors" at Focus on the Family, I served local churches as pastor. I began my ministry in a little church that was about to close, and completed it in a megachurch that, although it had a certain degree of dysfunction, was an influential congregation.

In those 30-plus years, I discovered a truth that should be very obvious but for some reason seems to be hidden in all the church growth publications and dialog: *Men matter!* The more active that men are in a local congregation, the more vibrant the church will be. The more active the role a father takes in the parenting of his children, the more likely that child will carry on the spiritual heritage of the family.

In David T. Olson's book *The American Church in Crisis*, he revealed a sobering study of the church in Switzerland. "If a father does not go to church, no matter how regular the mother is in her religious practice, only one child in 50 becomes a regular church attender" (89). That statistic says so much about the condition of the church in that country but has ramifications for churches everywhere. You men who rationalize your significance as a spiritual role model to your families are sorely mistaken. Look at your close friends. Take stock of their families, and you'll see how crucial the man of the house is to the development of a child's faith.

In my booklet *The Pastor's Role in Establishing an Effective Men's Ministry,* I quoted from George Barna: "If the church is to stem the tide of biblical illiteracy and waning commitment to the Christian faith, men will have to establish themselves as partners and leaders of the spiritual function of families. The apparent lack of spiritual leadership exhibited by millions of Christian men has hampered the spiritual growth of tens of thousands of well-meaning but spiritually inept families" (News release, Barna Group Ltd.).

Wow! You're the gatekeeper for the moral, spiritual, and emotional development of your home. You must be intentional. Because your job requires travel, and you're spending time away from your children, intentionality becomes even more important. It's not so much a matter of teaching as it is living. You do not need to be a great scholar to train your children properly, but you must live your life in such a way that your family will "catch" and apply the value and priority system that you establish.

The familiar passage from Proverbs 22:6 as paraphrased in *The Message* says, "Point your kids in the right direction—when they're old they won't be lost." Three words underscore the truth of that one verse—influence, attitude, example.

Men, you really do matter! You make a difference. Go for it! 📖

---

*H. B. London Jr. is the vice president of church & clergy at Focus on the Family.*

# MY BODY, HIS TEMPLE

STUART CAMPBELL ··········································································

*Don't you know that you yourselves are God's temple and that God's Spirit lives in you? If anyone destroys God's temple, God will destroy him; for God's temple is sacred, and you are that temple* (1 Corinthians 3:16-17).

Having been raised in a strict Southern Baptist family, I've always been familiar with the biblical truth that when you give your life to Christ and the Holy Spirit comes to live in you, your body becomes the temple of God. 1 Corinthians 3:16-17 was often quoted around the dinner table when the topic turned to the evils of drugs, alcohol, and tobacco. However, the conversation tended to stop there, and there was little discussion about how overeating and lack of exercise might fit into that same picture.

I have always struggled with maintaining a healthy weight and have gone through phases in my life when I was successful in that regard—and phases where I have failed miserably. I'm generally a disciplined person, so my lack of discipline around food and exercise has been a continual source of embarrassment for me.

That's just it. I've always viewed my being overweight from the perspective of my pride. I know that overweight people are almost always less physically attractive than their right-sized counterparts. There's little motivation to wear the latest men's fashions when nothing really looks very good on a 240-pound, 5'9" frame. Hanging out in the hotel pool with the kids loses some of its charm when you see your not-so-flattering reflection in the wading pool. So why was this never enough motivation to eat right and exercise?

I guess for me it took the realization that my body is really not my own, that it's a gift that should be treated with tender-loving care. One day God will provide me with a glorified body (1 Corinthians 15:35-58), but in the meantime, it's my job to make the most of the one He gave me. The Bible is clear on the virtues of self-control (Galatians 5:22) and the evils of gluttony (Ezekiel 16:49). But ultimately, it was the realization that God has given me a wonderful wife and two great boys who depend on me, and that I have a biblical obligation to set an example for them and raise them in the ways of the Lord (Ephesians 6:4).

So I've now lost 45 pounds, have gone down several pants sizes, no longer have heartburn, have knees that no longer give me trouble, have energy to go on long walks with my wife, and can keep up with my boys. And I love it! Isn't it amazing how much better life works when we do things God's way instead of our own?

Most hotels and motels nowadays have small exercise rooms. Why not get into the habit of using them? 📖

---

*Stuart Campbell is a retired president of Blue Cross and Blue Shield of Missouri and Wisconsin.*

# SHARING THE WALK

AL COLE ·····························································

*Two are better than one, because they have a good return for their work: if one falls down, his friend can help him up. But pity the man who falls and has no one to help him up! (Ecclesiastes 4:9-10).*

To many men, "accountability" is a dirty word. An acquaintance of mine put it this way: "I'm already accountable to my wife, my kids, and my boss. The last thing I need is one more person telling me I'm not living up to my potential as a husband, father, or—worst of all—a disciple of Christ."

On the surface, it seems like a reasonable complaint. But it misses the point. The idea behind being accountable to another guy on your Christian walk isn't merely to have someone else around to point out your flaws. Ideally, the focus of an accountability partner should be to help us be honest with ourselves, to keep us from rationalizing behaviors that might lead us away from God. As it says in Jeremiah 17:9, "The heart is deceitful above all things."

Pastor Rick Warren of Saddleback Church and author of *The Purpose-Driven Life* says we were created to live in community with one another, not in isolation. "No man is an island" is the way the poet John Donne put it hundreds of years ago. And deep down we know this is true, even though we sometimes buy into the lone-wolf image glamorized in those old spaghetti westerns.

In my own life I've tried it both ways. I've gone the route of the lone wolf, but more recently I've tried surrendering my pride and letting another guy get to know the real me, the man I see in the mirror every day. I'm not saying this is easy—it certainly doesn't come naturally—but I can assure you it's a lot better than trying to tough things out alone.

No matter what my friend and I are discussing, we often wind up asking each other such things as "Where is God in this situation?" or "What does God want me to learn here?" Of course, we can ask these kinds of questions when we're alone—and I still do at times—but asking them in the presence of another Christian man who knows me as I truly am is different. When we share our hopes, fears, and struggles with one another in this way, God delivers His comfort and encouragement through us. ▮▮▮

---

*Al Cole is executive director of National Coalition for the Protection of Children & Families in Atlanta.*

# THE SECRET TO OVERCOMING FEAR

DAVID GRAVES ························································

*Do not be afraid of those who kill the body but cannot kill the soul. Rather, be afraid of the One who can destroy both soul and body in hell. Are not two sparrows sold for a penny? Yet not one of them will fall to the ground apart from the will of your Father. And even the very hairs of your head are all numbered. So don't be afraid; you are worth more than many sparrows* (Matthew 10:28-31).

Fear is a common thing for everyone. I guess all of us are afraid of something. Some of us fear failure. Some of us fear being left alone. Some of us fear death. Some of us disguise our fear better than others, but fear can make our lives miserable.

In Matthew 10:28-31 Jesus gives us words of encouragement and help when it comes to fear. He uses the analogy of tiny sparrows. This awesome God whom we're to fear is also the God who cares about the smallest sparrow. In Christ's day, *sparrows* were the cheapest type of living food sold in the market; a *penny* was the smallest copper coin. Sparrows were not of high value in the world—a penny could buy two of them. Yet God is so concerned for them that *not one* falls to the ground without His consent. God marks the sparrow every time it lights and hops upon the ground.

Not only does God see the sparrows—He even knows the number of *the very hairs on our heads.* He's concerned about the most trifling details about each of us. Because God is aware of everything that happens to us, Jesus concludes that His followers need never be afraid.

We're so valuable that God sent Jesus, His only Son, to die for us (John 3:16). Because God places such value on us, we need never fear personal threats or difficult trials. God our Father is in control. He sees the sparrow fall; He knows and controls everything that happens to us. God cares not only about the big problems and situations of life but also about the tiniest details.

Early in the spring of 1905, Civilla Martin and her husband were spending some time in Elmira, New York. They developed a deep friendship with a couple we know only as Mr. and Mrs. Doolittle. Mrs. Doolittle had been bedridden for nearly 20 years, and her husband was confined to a wheelchair. Despite their afflictions, they lived happy Christian lives and brought inspiration and comfort to all who knew them.

One day while visiting with the Doolittles, Civilla's husband commented on their bright hopefulness and asked them for the secret of it. Mrs. Doolittle's reply was simple: "His eye is on the sparrow, and I know He watches me." The beauty of this simple expression of faith gripped Civilla Martin's heart, and she wrote a poem that she mailed the next day to Charles Gabriel, who put music to it.

Singer Ethel Waters made the resulting song famous, so famous that she used its name as the title for her autobiography. Perhaps you have heard the song:

*Why should I feel discouraged?*
  *Why should the shadows come?*
*Why should my heart be lonely*
  *And long for heaven and home*
*When Jesus is my portion?*
  *My constant friend is He.*
*His eye is on the sparrow,*
  *And I know He watches me.*
*I sing because I'm happy;*
  *I sing because I'm free.*
*For His eye is on the sparrow,*
  *And I know He watches me.*
*"Let not your heart be troubled,"*
  *His tender words I hear;*
*And resting on His goodness,*
  *I lose my doubt and fear.*
*Tho' by the path He leadeth*
  *But one step I may see,*
*His eye is on the sparrow*
  *And I know He watches me.*

Fear not—the Lord is with you!

---

*David Graves is senior pastor of College Church of the Nazarene, Olathe, Kansas.*

# LISTENING TO GOD

RICHARD E. JOHNSON ·····························································

*Show me your ways, O Lord, teach me your paths; guide me in your truth and teach me, for you are God my Savior, and my hope is in you all day long* (Psalm 25:4-5).

I was walking to the end of the island with my wife, along with my cousin and his wife. My cousin and I had both "married into" family cottages on different island communities, and we were enjoying comparing notes on the many humorous experiences and attitudes we had had. It was a glorious September day with just a bit of crispness in the air as the island began to anticipate fall. We had been enjoying the lush crop of blackberries along the path to the south shore.

As we rounded a bend in the path, just before it opened onto the rocky coast, I noticed a young girl sitting on a bench, looking out to sea. I had never met her, yet I felt a slight urge to approach her. Without a word or even a debate in my mind, I left my guests and went over to where she was sitting. After I said hello, we introduced ourselves and noted the respective cottages and families we were connected to. Her knees were drawn up with her feet on the bench, and I saw a book under her legs. I asked what she was reading.

"The Bible."

"Why?"

She told me that she had just become a Christian, led to the Lord through the ministry of Young Life. She was going to be starting college in a week or so, and here on the island she was enjoying the end of her summer vacation. I asked her if there were others in her family who were believers. She said there were none. There was no one in her family who was going to be praying for her. I told her I would.

The encounter lasted no more than two or three minutes. Was it an important encounter? Here is why I think it was.

God blessed me in a very unique way. I struggle at times with my responsibility toward those in my family who are not believers or walking with the Lord. In this encounter God showed me once again that I am not necessarily part of the equation that leads to their salvation. He redeemed this young lady even though her family was not praying toward that end.

Secondly, I believe that she was blessed. Here, out of the blue, a stranger who was a believer stopped to say he would pray for her. In a small but tangible way, she saw that God would provide for her. From unexpected places, He will bring people into her life for support, mentoring, and good times.

The personal challenge for all of us is this: will we *show up* in life? Are we available to be part of God's plan, or are we so busy and caught up in our own lives that we only ask Him to bless us and our activities?

Take time to be quiet with God, even when you are on the road. Watch for those divine intersections. Listen to Him as you meditate on His word or His creation. Don't be in a rush and miss an opportunity to be part of what God wants to do in you or through you. ▮▮

---

*Richard E. Johnson is a physician in Dunbarton, New Hampshire.*

# HUMAN ACCLAIM

BRUCE FONG ·····················································································

It was a pleasure to be asked to join the speaking team of a very large ministry for a great stadium gathering. I was ushered into a back room and shown every courtesy. Once the preliminary briefing was complete, I had some down time, so I began to wander about.

One of my hosts invited me into a windowless room. The door was marked "Hospitality." A number of men were relaxing in this room. To the side was a table filled with beverages, snacks, and fruit.

Everyone in the room was cheerful and munching on something. I picked up a few refreshments, walked over to this gathering of strangers, sat in a folding chair, and flashed a friendly smile.

Each man in turn thrust out his hand and gave his name. To this day I would have to look up their individual names to remember who they were. Once the introductions were done, my host saw a puzzled look on my face and reintroduced this collection of four men as the amazingly talented men's quartet, 4Him.

We had great fellowship together. These men are celebrities yet were just ordinary men whose Christian walk was the most important priority for each of them.

After they left the room, one of the program producers commented that these guys are the real deal. They're as humble as they are talented. Their whole goal is to glorify the Lord with their singing.

Jesus highlighted this quality of humble service when He taught. He warned people to watch out for teachers who love human acclaim. They intentionally advance their reputation among men. Yet they're selfish and motivated to rise in popularity through religious habits.

Are you talented? Is human acclaim starting to rise for you? Keep humble. Practice your craft to bring attention to Him. When we do this, He will lift us up!

Be encouraged in God's Word: Mark 12:35-40.   ◼

---

*Bruce Fong is president of Michigan Theological Seminary in Plymouth, Michigan.*

# THE NEED FOR A HEART CHANGE

DAVID GRAVES ·····················································

*The heart is deceitful above all things and beyond cure. Who can understand it? "I the LORD search the heart and examine the mind, to reward a man according to his conduct, according to what his deeds deserve"* (Jeremiah 17:9-10).

In December 1967 doctors performed the first human heart transplant. The operation was performed by a team of surgeons headed by Christiaan N. Barnard in Cape Town, South Africa. The patient, 53-year-old dentist Louis Washkansky, was given the heart of a 25-year-old auto crash victim named Denise Darvall. Washkansky died from infection 18 days later, but the transplant made Barnard one of the world's most famous surgeons. During the next several years, many individuals with diseased and damaged hearts also received transplants.

Spiritually, we all are in need of heart transplants. Our spiritual hearts are diseased and damaged. God makes it clear why we sin—it's a matter of the heart. Our hearts have been inclined toward sin from the time we were born. Our hearts are deceitful, crooked, polluted.

Truly, the core of every problem lies in the human heart that is deceitful and incurable. We often say, "Well, if I know my own heart . . ." But we *don't* know our own hearts. If we want to know what our hearts are like, we must read the Word and let the Holy Spirit teach us.

Even though we don't know our hearts, God does. He searches the heart and examines the mind. He knows that the human heart is basically selfish and that the human mind focuses primarily on itself; but though people justifiably love themselves, they fail to love their neighbors as themselves. No amount of righteous deeds can make someone acceptable to God, for no one can achieve perfect righteousness by his or her own efforts.

Our only hope is new hearts. Only God can perform a spiritual heart transplant, and He wants to give us new hearts. In Ezekiel 36:26-27, God promises, "I will give you a new heart and put a new spirit in you; I will remove from you your heart of stone and give you a heart of flesh. And I will put my Spirit in you and move you to follow my decrees and be careful to keep my laws." Our Heavenly Father is a heart specialist—He is our Great Physician. ▮▮

---

*David Graves is senior pastor of College Church of the Nazarene, Olathe, Kansas.*

# OUR SEXUALIZED CULTURE

BILL SHIPLEY

Ours is a sexualized culture that offers temptation to men in the areas that are part of our everyday lives. Computers, television, movies, plus advertisements in all types of media show that suggestive pictures are more risqué than ever before. When we travel, there are always pornographic movies available in the privacy of our hotel and motel rooms. If we have a weakness in the area of pornography, all of this can work against what we're supposed to be, and especially what God wants us to be.

There's something in our human nature that doesn't want to face the reality that we live in two worlds. We live in the physical world where we have jobs, use our computers, watch movies, read books, and go about our daily business. We also live in a spiritual world, and *that world is at war!*

Ron Hutchcraft (Ron Hutchcraft Ministries) puts it this way: "Sadly, what happens to snowmen seems to be happening to more and more of God's people. They're slowly going soft, melted by the heat of a culture that applies heavy pressure to compromise both Christian convictions and Christian lifestyles. And some of us are becoming so melted that you can hardly tell the difference between us and the lost people around us."

1 Peter 2:11 warns, "Abstain from sinful desires, which war against the soul." These are wrong desires that literally start a war in our souls. Whatever feeds those destructive desires in our minds and hearts is something that we can't afford, no matter how exciting or how interesting it appears to be.

That's why God says the strategy for keeping our soul from being poisoned is very simple—*abstain*. Stay away from sinful desires and the influences that feed them. In fact, as 2 Timothy 2:22 says, "Flee the evil desires of youth, and pursue righteousness, faith, love and peace, along with those who call on the Lord out of a pure heart."

As men, we must remember that there are things that other people are watching and doing that we and they can't afford to watch or do. These areas can cause our hearts to harden. There are things we cannot afford to listen to, places we cannot afford to go, material we cannot afford to read, and web sites we should never visit. These are areas that damage our souls and our lives as well as the lives of others we touch.

Provocative images, suggestive humor, sexual scenes and themes get into our thought systems and stay there for years. We never seem to forget them. Wrong desires slowly start to dominate so many of our thoughts. Without our even realizing it, we reach a point where we can't help thinking wrong, thinking sin. If we're married, these moral issues dilute and pollute our focus on the one person we should be directing all of our desire to—our "loved one." Job 31:1 says, "I made a covenant with my eyes not to look lustfully at a girl."

The Bible says that it's possible to "take captive every thought to make it obedient to Christ" (2 Corinthians 10:5). But we must set boundaries that will keep out the vile messages that are all over the Internet, our TV screens, our hotel rooms, our radios, and magazines, books and CDs. It's a battle to keep these messages out of our systems, and it's a battle for moral conviction that is worth fighting. 📖

---

*Bill Shipley is president of Shipley Enterprises, Charlotte, North Carolina.*

# DON'T QUIT!
# A SON'S HUMILITY THAT LEADS

JASPER HALL 〰〰〰〰〰〰〰〰〰〰〰〰〰〰〰〰〰〰〰〰〰〰〰〰〰〰〰〰〰〰〰〰〰〰〰〰〰〰〰〰

*Fathers, do not embitter your children or they will become discouraged* (Colossians 3:21).

It was a typical spring morning when the family and I hurriedly loaded the car with drinks, snacks, shin guards, socks, and Nintendo DS games. Yes, we were headed to our day of soccer in our local recreational league. I called it a "day of soccer," because with three children and at least two games to play, it was definitely going to be a "day of." As the coach, I had slated my oldest son, Joshua, who is a sensitive, loving, and caring young man of 11, to play goalie.

He was moderately excited, because outside of practice, he hadn't really ever played a position. In his previous season, soccer looked more like "amoeba ball," in which every child attacked the ball and had no regard for positions.

But on this day it was different. There was no score in the first couple of periods, and while shaky at times, Joshua managed to hold his own and save a couple of shots on goal. Then came the final period. All of a sudden our team really started to struggle to keep up with the other team. We found ourselves constantly trying to defend our goal, and Joshua was increasingly getting nervous.

Then suddenly—*score!* One shot had slipped by Joshua. That was okay. We had heard this team was really talented and might be a tough opponent. Then almost immediately—another goal! The parents were cheering, and the other players were celebrating and even jeering at our kids. This went on for what seemed like 30 minutes, in which time they scored six goals to our zero. I have to admit that I was sad and discouraged for our team, but especially for Joshua. I—as well as my wife and a few others—were all trying to yell instructions for him at the same time; I'm sure it came across only as a loud noise to him.

When Joshua returned to the sidelines, he was fighting back tears. He did not want to discuss what had just happened. We did the typical mom-and-dad thing by pointing out how well he had done by holding off the other team for almost the whole game. Deep down, of course, I was embarrassed and sad for him.

We practiced the next week, and before we knew it Saturday had arrived, bringing with it another game. Joshua said, "Dad, I want to play goalie!" I asked if he was sure, and he confidently affirmed it. I reluctantly gave both my permission and a few more pointers. That day my son stopped every ball that came near the goalie box. He was tenacious and aggressive, which typically wasn't even his style. He remained serious and never really looked to the sidelines. He didn't say a word the entire game until the end, when he remarked, "I think I really like being a goalie, Dad!"

That night, as I made the rounds to pray with my children, I headed toward Joshua's room. I was almost in tears when I looked in his face and said, "Joshua, I can't begin to tell you how proud I was of you today. You showed something today that many young men or women your age would never have shown. It was great courage and humility. You demonstrated what it means to not quit, and that also says a lot about your character."

After he thanked me, I added, "Joshua all the things I just said really were much more about you than the way you played soccer last weekend or today. The fact is, you showed great leadership not only for your teammates but also for the parents and coaches, and most of all for me. Thank you, son. I love you." We prayed, and he went on to bed. I walked away having realized that I had truly just seen Jesus in my son and seen him be the kind of leader I always need to be.

The scriptures are very clear here with instructions to fathers on how we are to be with our children (Colossians 3:20). We should always encourage and never provoke or embitter (which means to make bitter). The practical application to our lives, however, is that as fathers, husbands, and men, we need to be models of obedience to God and let all our actions please Him.  ▐▌▌

---

*Jasper Hall is a board member for National Coalition for the Protection of Children & Families.*

# A FAMILY UNITED IN CHRIST

GEORGE D. MCKINNEY ·····················································

*When Jesus saw his mother there, and the disciple whom he loved standing nearby, he said to his mother, "Dear woman, here is your son"* (John 19:26).

In the divine drama of redemption, God has often used families and communities to fulfill His purpose. God chose Noah and his family to begin the process of repopulating the earth. Later He called Abraham and his family to be the instruments through whom redemption would come to all nations of the earth. Still later He used Jacob and his family to preserve His people and demonstrate His sovereignty among the nations.

Even at the scene of the Cross prior to Jesus' death, God reaffirmed the importance of family relationships. Although Jesus had reached the culminating moment of His life and ministry, the significance of His suffering and death did not cause Him to deny or discount His family relationships. On the contrary, the mutual love, respect, and affection between mother and Son were evident even then—especially then—in His dying moments. Their deep devotion had been formed in the crucible of suffering—the knowledge of His ultimate ordeal (Luke 2:35)—and in their mutual hope and expectation of His mission.

In the final moments of His life, Jesus was comforted not only by the presence of His mother but also by other members of the family of faith, including John, the beloved disciple, and Mary Magdalene. In this critical moment of His impending death, Jesus gathered members of His biological and spiritual family into a new community. As He died, He exclaimed, "Woman, behold thy son!" John, the beloved disciple, assumed the role of son to Mary and welcomed her into his household.

Mary Magdalene and others at the Cross were drawn together by the community experience of grief and disappointment. But at that moment at the Cross and later at the empty tomb, the seeds of community were planted that would burst forth into new life at Pentecost.

At the very center of this community, the family was drawn together by the Savior at the moment of His death. He drew it together as a promise of the family of God who were to grow even "unto the ends of the earth" (Acts 13:47), a community reconciled to God in Christ, who share the ministry of reconciliation (2 Corinthians 5:18).

As you travel, consider not only those who are your biological family but also those who are your spiritual family. Pray for them and for the Lord's guidance in your life for your role among them. ▮▮▮

---

*George D. McKinney is jurisdictional prelate and general board member of the Church of God in Christ, Inc., San Diego.*

# WOMEN HAVE FRIENDS— MEN HAVE WIVES

**DAN REXROTH** ·····················································

As men, we often pride ourselves in our autonomy. "Independent," "rugged individualist," and "self-sufficient" are badges generally viewed as positive male traits. Our relationships typically revolve around wife and family. We may have a few connections with other guys through hobbies, sports or other pastimes, but most of those tend to be rather superficial. Men don't feel they need other men.

Men are focused on getting things done. We love to solve problems and check things off our "to do" list. It promotes a sense of accomplishment and importance. We love to conquer. Life, however, is not about accomplishment but rather relationship. We should pause, reflect, and correct this misconception. Most important is our relationship to God, then to others. In Matthew 22:36-40, Jesus boils all of Scripture down when He gives us the two greatest commandments. He said, "Love the Lord your God with all your heart . . . and your neighbor as yourself."

In the Body of Christ, the lack of meaningful relationships between men is the elephant in the room most of us don't talk about. The ability to share burdens, grow and challenge each other in our faith, hold each other accountable, and mentor and be mentored to are all benefits of male relationships. These kinds of relationships are especially important to men who spend large amounts of time away from home where temptation can be hidden. Proverbs 27:17 says, "As iron sharpens iron, so one man sharpens another."

Christ does not call us to anything we can't accomplish with His help. Real relationships with other men may feel difficult and unnatural for many of us. But because Christ has put such an emphasis on our relationships within the Body, we're compelled to obey.

Express to Him your need for help in this area of your life. Once you acknowledge your dependence on Him to build relationships, things will start happening. Actually, building a positive, healthy relationship with God is a big step toward building positive, healthy relationships with others.

Make it a priority to build spiritual relationships with a few other men in your life. Discuss with Him your desire to have a close friend. It takes work to build that kind of relationship. You may be thinking you don't have the time, you'll be vulnerable, and it doesn't feel comfortable. All these things may be true. It is, however, critically important to being the kind of growing, maturing believer Christ wants you to be.

In his book *The Purpose-Driven Life* Rick Warren says, "It is not enough just to say relationships are important; we must prove it by investing time in them." *O Lord, help us men to use our time for what you say is important in life.*

---

*Dan Rexroth is president and CEO of Premier Life/John Knox Village, Lenexa, Kansas.*

# THE POWER OF WORDS

DALE HARLOW ·····································································

*"Then neither do I condemn you," Jesus declared. "Go now and leave your life of sin"* (John 8:11).

The date was June 22, 1996. Jordan had turned 10 the day before and was having several of his friends over for a party. The highlight of any birthday party is opening the presents. Our eight-year-old son had gone out a few days before and bought a gift for the party. Our two youngest had not bought presents. That was fine with us because Jordan didn't need a present from them. We didn't think it would ever be an issue. It wasn't, at least not until the day of the party.

They both went through their own things until they could find a treasure to give to their brother. Taylor came up with a Happy Meal toy that was better than most Happy Meal toys. But still—it was a *Happy Meal toy.* We knew it didn't matter to Jordan, and it sure did not matter to us. Jordan opened presents that 10-year-olds love: a sports jersey, a sports hat, another sports hat, and, well—you get the picture.

Then he came to Taylor's gift. When the toy dropped out of the wrapping paper, one of the boys said, "It's a Happy Meal toy!" and all of them started to laugh. Taylor immediately put both hands over his face in embarrassment. But Jordan, showing wisdom beyond his single decade, said, "Hey, neat!" and started to play with it. The laughter quickly stopped, and Jordan soon went on to the next gift.

After all the presents were opened, two of the other boys came over and started to play with the Happy Meal toy. It wasn't that the Happy Meal toy looked any more appealing than when it was opened, but they realized what Jordan had done, and they wanted to follow suit.

In the story in John 8, what could have been more embarrassing than being dragged from the bed of adultery into the public square? But that's exactly what happened when they threw the unnamed adulteress at the feet of the Carpenter. I picture her with two hands over her face, realizing that her future was in the hands of those around her. Imagine the combination of arrogance and hate of those holding the rocks.

But then something amazing happened. Jesus came up with one mirror for each stone—and suddenly sin had a different face.

What turned arrogant hatred into humility? They saw what those 10-year-old boys saw. They saw a man reach out in love and remove the hands that covered the face of embarrassment. They saw the love of Jesus transfer embarrassment from the broken to the arrogant. The transfer causes men to drop rocks, and boys to play with a toy in which they have no interest.

I must admit that I never caught Jordan playing with that toy again. But he did play with it long enough to let a child know that the little brother meant more to him than the attitude of his friends.

What are you doing to heal the hurting and lift up the broken? Are you throwing stones, or are you empathetically entering into the souls of those with whom you come in contact?   📖

---

*Dale Harlow is senior pastor of Northfield Christian Church in Ft. Dodge, Iowa.*

# MAKE NO FRIENDS WITH AN ANGRY MAN

ALEX MCFARLAND ·····························································

Proverbs 15:1 says that "A gentle answer turns away wrath, but a harsh word stirs up anger." When it comes to resolving differences with people, Benjamin Franklin was right when he said "an ounce of prevention is worth a pound of cure."

A journalist and I were once having a friendly conversation. Upon hearing that I had been ordained a Baptist minister, she asked me, "What's the difference between a Baptist preacher and a steel beam?" When she answered, "Steel beams are flexible," I had to laugh. But I also winced slightly at the knowledge that all too often Christians have a negative but well-deserved reputation of being stubborn. Should we have convictions? Absolutely. Would Jesus have us be abrasive and argumentative? I don't think so.

As we serve the Lord and prepare for even greater areas of service, we must remember that we're called to be peacemakers.

Getting along with others in the business world is not always easy. Doing so does not mean that we compromise truth, but often the way we carry ourselves or deal gently with others will make a wonderfully positive impact on the outcome of a discussion.

For years our society has become increasingly litigious. Court dockets are filled with lawsuits of every kind as individuals and companies fight out their differences. When we deal with others honestly, forthrightly, and make good on our promises, legal recourse is rarely, if ever, necessary.

When working as an attorney, Abraham Lincoln let everyone know he did not approve of petty litigation and minor lawsuits. You may just imagine how he felt the day an angry businessman approached him, intent on suing a bankrupt debtor who owed him $2.50 for an unpaid bill.

Lincoln tried to talk the businessman out of filing a case over such a trivial amount, but the man refused to be stopped. So Lincoln agreed and asked for a $10 retainer fee. The client, bent on filing a case, agreed.

After he took the money, Lincoln sought out the bankrupt defendant and gave him half. With the $5 windfall in hand, the defendant agreed to pay the debt and settle the matter. The plaintiff was victorious. The defendant now had a little money in his pocket. And Lincoln was able to avert an unnecessary lawsuit.

We should endeavor to follow John's words "He [Jesus] must increase, but I must decrease" (John 3:30, KJV). There is way too much to be done for God's glory to be entangled by the methods of the world. Let's yield our emotions to Christ and invest our energies in the Father's business. ▮▮▮

---

*Alex McFarland is president of Southern Evangelical Seminary in Matthews, North Carolina.*

# FAITHFUL IN THE SMALL THINGS

MIKE PLATTER ·······························································

*He who had received five talents came and brought five other talents, saying, "Lord, you delivered to me five talents; look, I have gained five more talents besides them." His lord said to him, "Well done, good and faithful servant; you were faithful over a few things, I will make you ruler over many things. Enter into the joy of your lord"* (Matthew 25:20-21, NKJV).

Just off Interstate 40 in Amarillo, Texas, is the Big Texan Steak Ranch. Since the mid-1960s they've offered an entrée that has made them famous: the 72-ounce steak. The current price for those 4½ pounds of beef with the dinner plate *(baked potato, salad, dinner roll, and shrimp cocktail)* is $73. But they'll give it to you free if you eat the entire dinner in one hour or less!

Since they started offering the deal, over 42,000 people have tried to eat the steak in the time limit. 8,000 have succeeded. Here are a few of the outstanding moments from the last 40 years:

The youngest winner was an 11-year-old boy. The oldest? A 69-year-old grandmother!

Klondike Bill, a professional wrestler in the 1960s, consumed 2 steaks in one hour.

Former Cincinnati Reds pitcher Frank Pastore holds the record for the fastest time: 9-1/2 minutes.

A married couple from Nevada have eaten the steak dinner at least 10 times since 1995. Both usually complete it in less than 30 minutes.

The reason that the Big Texan can give away all those free steaks is because they know that people will "bite off more than they can chew." At least five people attempt it for every one person who succeeds. That's human nature; but it also teaches us something about faithfulness.

Most of us are interested in the big accomplishments— the ones that make the headlines, the stories celebrated in sermons and in songs. But big moments and big achievements are rare, and to focus on them is to miss something far more important. The real stuff from which life is made is found in small moments and in little acts of achievement.

It is faithfulness in the small things that prepares you for any big moments that God may have planned for you. Jesus' 33 years of life did indeed contain great moments and achievements—but the first 30 years were not considered important enough for the Bible to record. Nevertheless, those years prepared Him for the great moments that have made all the difference for your life and the lives of those you love.

Thousands of people eat at Big Texan Steak Ranch every week—but only about 20 attempt the 72-ounce dinner special. We don't tell the stories of the average customers, but they're the ones who keep the restaurant going.

It's the same way with our faithfulness to God and to our families. Be faithful today: in the choices you make—in the things to which you say "yes" or "no"—to the prayers you offer for your family, and for God's blessing on your life. Make faithful choices—with God's help—in the small, hourly decisions of your life today. And when you add those moments all together, God will tell the story of your faithfulness and integrity. 

---

*Mike Platter is senior pastor of Glendora Community Church of the Nazarene.*

# IS THERE INFECTION PRESENT?

RICHARD E. JOHNSON ·····················································

*There is a way that seems right to a man, but in the end it leads to death*
(Proverbs 14:12).

I had an infection in my foot. It seemed to be under control and not interfering with my life. Then one afternoon, out of the blue, the infection and its poison spread throughout my body. I could feel myself rapidly getting weaker, and within six short hours I was hospitalized with septic shock.

We need to ask what seemingly small infections we tolerate in our lives. Are there evil things we know are there, but we think they're okay, under control, or even justified—things like a secret sin or addiction, a heart attitude, a negative way of relating to someone, our anger, our view of our own importance, unforgiveness, or an unrepentant spirit? Yes, we can live with some of this for a while. We're able to cover them over. Maybe we feel justified in our attitude, sin, or addiction. It does not appear to affect our life and interaction with others.

Life and reality, however, teach us otherwise. People think the cigarettes they smoke will not affect them because they feel fine now. Yet 430,000 die of smoking-related illness every year. We enjoy a drink of alcohol and eat fast food with its high sugar, fat, and chemicals, yet obesity and alcohol abuse are destroying lives.

In our lives we think that the little lie or half truth will not hurt anyone—it only makes us look better in the eyes of others. Unforgiveness poisons our view of others and leads us down the path of victimization. An unwillingness to repent keeps us from having a healthy relationship with our wives. Pornography may seem to be for our personal pleasure, yet it's a cancer that eats away at our abilities to relate intimately with our wives.

In our spiritual life we go along as if we don't need to be in God's presence. Saying grace at a meal is the extent of our prayer lives. Maybe we ask God to bless our plans for the day or the projects we're working on. But do we spend time listening to Him? Are we anxious to know what God wants and is doing, or are our plans more important? The truth is, more often than not, that we're in a state of spiritual anorexia.

The challenge is to be aware of the small, seemingly under-control infections in our lives. We need to identify them, treat them, and make sure they're gone. If we don't, they can lead to spiritual septic shock. 

---

*Richard Johnson is a physician in Dunbarton, New Hampshire.*

# 1 + 1 + 1 = 1

J. K. WARRICK ·······················································

*"Haven't you read," he replied, 'that at the beginning the Creator made them 'male and female,' and said, 'For this reason a man will leave his father and mother and be united to his wife, and the two will become one flesh'? So they are no longer two, but one. Therefore what God has joined together let man not separate"* (Matthew 19:4-6).

1 + 1 + 1 = 1. I have a friend who is fond of saying, "I am very fast at math—just not very accurate!" You might read my equation and think that about me. 1 + 1 + 1 = 1? How can that be?

In the classroom it might not make sense, but in marriage it makes all the sense in the world. One man + one woman + God = one great life! Bad math; good theology!

Patty and I have been married for 41 years. We've been together so long that I can tell you how she thinks about some things. For instance, if you ask me whether she would like to take a road trip with me on the Harley, well, the answer to that is "No, thanks!" She might go for a short ride, but her one long ride was enough for a lifetime.

However, if you were to ask me if she would like to drop by the mall for a while, I can tell you that she would readily say, "Absolutely—when do we go?" I know that she won't drink caffeine after lunch and she would rather have Tex-Mex food than about any other kind. She prefers Holiday Inn Express and will not stay in a smoking room unless there's just no choice. She always takes a "to go" drink at restaurants, and you just live with that. It is what it is!

Obviously, she could do the same for me. We are, well, we are just *one* in so many ways. Our lives are centered in Christ, and our love is bound up by His love. We won't drift apart, because our love is encircled by His love. You know—1 + 1 + 1 = 1!

I like it this way! She loves me. I love her. We love God in Christ. We're one in Him. It's a safe place for our love and a safe place for us. It's been a safe place for our children, and it's now a safe place for our grandchildren. Talk about security!

Just think: God had us (and you and your wife) in mind when He created this world. What a God! What a life! What a way to love and be loved!

Prayer: *Father, fill my heart with love for my wife, and give me grace to express that love to her in ways that will bless her and give her joy. In Jesus' name I pray. Amen.*

---

*J. K. Warrick is general superintendent of the International Church of the Nazarene.*

# DISCIPLINE THROUGH MODELING

JEFF PRATHER ·····················································

As a psychologist working with young people and parents, and even more so as a father myself, it's important for me to remember that *discipline* in its root form suggests *guidance*. Many parents have come to my office over the years to express their concern about the path of their son's or daughter's life. Commonly these parents talk about what they've done in an attempt to intervene with their children—grounding, taking away privileges, offering rewards.

I've also had the opportunity to talk with these young men and women themselves. As they shared with me their views of family and life, it became clear to me what was happening in many of these situations. These parents wanted their children to be healthy people, to have faith in God, but what was often missing was an appealing example for their children of what this looks like.

Research on modeling suggests that one of the determining factors as to whether someone will follow a model is how *appealing* the model is. We're all at least somewhat aware that our children are watching us. They're deciding whether how we act and what we live for is good. Many of the young adults mentioned above did not view the model of the adults in their lives as positive, despite the fact that many of the parents were active Christians.

I've also had the opportunity to meet young people who gladly follow the paths of their parents. When I speak to these kids, it quickly becomes apparent that they admire their parents. These parents have provided discipline in perhaps its strongest form—they provide models for what life is about, living for something that's real to them. It has been my experience that young people sense that the world—beauty, popularity, wealth—is not real. The problem is that often a true example of what *is* real is not offered.

A child who is given love and limits and is offered a model of faith and purpose is a child on the path to knowing meaning and joy in life.

As fathers, we need to be aware. We need to be aware to the fact that our children are tuned in to how we live our lives.

We need to be aware that our decisions matter to more than just ourselves. While you travel this month, think on such questions as *What does my child feel is important to me?* and *Why would my child want to be like me?* Awareness of how your life is affecting others is a critical step toward making decisions and creating action that your children are likely to follow. Even when we're not in our children's presence, we're influencing and shaping their futures. Our decisions will impact their lives forever. ▮▮▮

*Jerry Prahter is a psychologist specializing in children and families.*

# IN WHAT DO YOU PUT YOUR TRUST?

DICK TOWNER ·················································

*The Lord is a refuge for the oppressed, a stronghold in times of trouble* (Psalm 9:9).

While thinking about all the bad news around us recently, I found myself reading through as many verses as I could find that contained the word "trouble." At first glance this may sound like a depressing exercise. It turned out to be deeply encouraging. Read and reflect upon the following verses:

In the day of trouble he will keep me safe in his dwelling; he will hide me in the shelter of his tabernacle and set me high upon a rock (*Psalm 27:5*).

You are my hiding place; you will protect me from trouble and surround me with songs of deliverance (*Psalm 32:7*).

"Because he loves me," says the LORD, "I will rescue him; I will protect him, for he acknowledges my name. He will call upon me, and I will answer him; I will be with him in trouble, I will deliver him and honor him" *(Psalm 91:14-15)*.

It's in times like this that we're led to re-evaluate what it is in which we place our trust. When things are in economic turmoil, we're inclined to say, "These are such economically uncertain times." And yet Scripture would seem to indicate that *all* times are economically uncertain, for our treasures on earth are always subject to the effects of rust and moths and thieves (and economic downturns!).

What is it in which you place your confidence? What do you believe will help you in a time of trouble? Andy Stanley suggests a question to ask ourselves that will reveal where we're placing our trust. Here's the question—reflect upon it: *Would you be more upset if you found out tomorrow that there was no God—or that you had no money in any of your bank accounts?*

When troubles come, as they inevitably will, remember God's promise that He will never leave us nor forsake us (Joshua 1:5). He is "our refuge and strength, an ever-present help in trouble" (Psalm 46:1).  ▮▮

---

*Dick Towner is executive director of Good $ense Stewardship Movement, Elgin, Illinois.*

# WHO IS EVALUATING YOUR LIFE?

STEVE WILSON ·····················································

For the past 10 years every aspect of my avocation has been under close scrutiny and evaluation. You see, I'm an official for the National Football League. The future of my career is determined by individuals who review my performance during each game. They're tasked with watching the details of *every* play and judge whether or not I made the right or wrong call. How would you like it if someone evaluated every phone call you made, every mile you drove, every detail of every product you produced? I came to the conclusion long ago that I had to prepare myself mentally, physically, and emotionally to use the gifts and skills God gave me to perform my job well.

What does God think about your future? We find the answer in Jeremiah 29:11—"I know the plans I have for you, declares the Lord, plans to prosper you and not to harm you, plans to give you hope and a future." Everything that characterizes our lives—the good, the bad, and the ugly—has been determined by our thoughts and our beliefs. What you have become has been shaped by the price you paid to get what you desired.

**Time out:** *Are you following a plan for your life? Is it God's plan?*

1. *Trust God with every detail of your life.* Most of the important battles we face are internal struggles, waged within ourselves. Nothing great has ever been achieved except by those who dared to believe that God was superior to any circumstance faced. 1 John 4:4 says, "The one who is in you is greater than the one who is in the world."

2. *Seek to live life with a positive attitude.* Don't put water in your own boat—the storms of life will put enough in on its own! Don't dream up thousands of reasons you can't achieve your goals; find one reason you can. It's easier to do all the things you should do than to spend the rest of your life wishing you had. The first key to victory is that you must win the battle over yourself. Zig Ziglar believes, "You can't consistently perform in a manner that is inconsistent with the way you see yourself."

3. *Form habits that will build your character.* Don't be your own worst enemy! This habit is like a microscope—-it magnifies the very *minute* things but cannot focus on the great ones. To keep from constantly beating yourself up, practice these simple steps daily: *multiply* your prayer time, *divide* the truth from the lies, *subtract* negative influences, and *add* God's Word. We lie loudest when we lie to ourselves. Both faith and fear may sail into your harbor, but allow only faith to drop anchor.

**Time out:** *Give thanks for God's grace and mercy in your life. Give thanks for your family, and seek His counsel in all aspects of your life.* 🛄

---

*Steve Wilson is an NFL official and executive pastor of Spokane Valley Church of the Nazarene, Spokane Valley, Washington.*

# BEARING OUR CROSS

THEO NICOLAKIS · · · · · · · · · · · · · · · · · · · · · · · · · · · · · · · · · · · · · · · · · · · · · · · · · · · · · · · · · · · · · · · ·

*He said to them all, "If anyone would come after me, he must deny himself and take up his cross daily and follow me"* (Luke 9:23).

My parish priest once told a parable about a man who felt that the literal cross he was carrying was heavier than it should be. So he went to the old man who made all the crosses and explained his predicament. The cross-maker seemed very understanding of the man's plight and offered him what sounded like a reasonable solution. "Why don't you go down into the storeroom and try all the crosses that are there? Select the one you prefer, the one that is the lightest, and leave your cross in its place." The young man did as he was told.

The man soon found himself trying various crosses. Now some crosses seemed to be quite light when compared to others but were still very heavy. After trying several hundred, he finally found one that was lighter than all the rest. Emerging from the storeroom, he asked the cross-maker if he could take the cross he was carrying.

"Of course," replied the cross-maker. "It's the one you were carrying when you first came to see me."

We know from Scripture that Christ calls each of us to deny himself or herself, take up his or her cross, and follow Him. Many times we might feel as though our own burdens outweigh those of others. I've experienced this feeling firsthand with my youngest child, who was born with a rare genetic disorder and has had special needs since birth. This condition ultimately led my wife and me to Boston Children's Hospital to seek specialized treatment for him.

It was a humbling experience to see other children of all ages coping with conditions of a far graver nature than my son's. In talking with some of the parents, I was amazed at how they were able to handle what I perceived as such an incredible burden. Like the man in the parable, I realized that there is no person—not a single one—who does not have a burden to bear. Others have triumphed over even greater adversity than my own.

I'm reminded that Paul suffered a "thorn in the flesh." Three times he asked God to take this affliction from him, and God responded, "My grace is sufficient for you, for my power is made perfect in weakness" (2 Corinthians 12:9). When Christ was weighed down by His cross, the Romans forced Simon of Cyrene to help carry it.

No matter where we find ourselves in life, no matter what adversity we face, no matter how desperate our situation may seem, there's no burden too difficult for us to bear. In those times when we feel we're stumbling and can no longer rise up and carry our cross, we're assured that Christ himself is there to walk with us.   ▐▊▐

---

*Theo Nicolakis is director of information technology for the Greek Orthodox Archdiocese of America.*

# THE DIFFERENCE

TOM TRASK ·····································································

Every four years athletes from around the world gather to compete for the goal of receiving a medal, preferably a gold medal. What sets these men and women apart from the millions of other athletes who, for a number of reasons, never attain to the level of an Olympic athlete? I believe it can be summed up in what I call the "3 Ds."

## DIVINE—DESIRE—DISCIPLINE

The first D is *divine*. When describing the Christian life as a race and what must happen to win, Paul the Apostle wrote, "Brothers, I do not consider myself yet to have taken hold of it. But one thing I do: Forgetting what is behind and straining toward what is ahead, I press on toward the goal to win the prize for which God has called me heavenward in Christ Jesus" (Phil. 3:13-14).

When you become a follower of Jesus Christ, you must believe you've been set apart. God's divine hand is upon you. His help, His enabling, His grace, and His strength are accessible to everyone who makes this decision to be a disciple of the Lord Jesus Christ.

One must know and be convinced that He wants you be a winner. God has made all His resources available to you.

The second D is *desire*. Some say it this way: "You gotta want to." In order for this to take place, one must forget the failures. Paul states that in verse 13: "Forgetting what is behind."

Second, one must persevere. Winners never quit.

In that same verse Paul says, "reaching forth unto those things which are before" (kjv). One must never be satisfied with the status quo. Stay on the *stretch*, reaching forth. A wonderful prize is waiting for all those who finish (Philippians 3:14).

The third D is for *discipline*. The athlete who makes it to the Olympic team has learned that he or she must be a person of discipline. Olympic athletes are willing to deny themselves some of the joys that the regular athletes have, such as what they do with their time, what they eat, and with whom they keep company. What are some of the values and disciplines a Christian must hold onto?

Here are some disciplines for men who are in a race to win:

1. Say *no* to temptation.
2. Be careful to have a *daily* devotional time.
   a. Read the Word of God daily.
   b. Take time to pray daily.
3. Be *faithful* to attend the house of the Lord and have fellowship with those who are in the same "race" for eternal life.
4. Be a *witness* of Jesus Christ.
5. Be a person of *conviction*. Romans 12:2 says, "Do not conform any longer to the pattern of this world, but be transformed by the renewing of your mind. Then you will be able

to test and approve what God's will is—His good, pleasing and perfect will."

Set your goal to be a "gold medal" Christian!

---

*Tom Trask is president of CrossExamined.org.*

# ENGAGE WITH GOD

JON KITNA

*Alarmed, Jehoshaphat resolved to inquire of the Lord. . . . "We do not know what to do, but our eyes are upon you"* (2 Chronicles 20:3, 12).

When we think of the "real men" in the Bible, we often come up with the names of David, Samson, Peter, Abraham, Noah, and so on. One of the names you won't hear very often is that of Jehoshaphat. How wrong we would be to not learn what it means to be a "REAL" man of God from this king!

In this passage we find Jehoshaphat discovering that three different people groups have joined forces as an army and are advancing against Israel. Upon hearing this news, we see a true response of a "REAL" man. He didn't consult his commanders or seek the council of his advisors. He didn't count his army or rouse his troops. He immediately engaged God in prayer. He declared a fast for the whole country with the purpose of hearing how God wanted them to fight this battle. Then he led the country in prayer, concluding with the realization—"We do not know what to do, but our eyes are upon you."

The overwhelming majority of us men, if we're honest, would say our prayer or attitudes toward God are more like this: *Lord, I've done everything I can think of, and things sure are a mess. Could you please wave your hand over things and make them better?* What I see in most men today is an attitude that regards men who are prayerful and who seek godly wisdom in all areas of their lives as weak. What we must do is learn from Jehoshaphat and develop a strong relationship with our Lord.

To have a strong relationship with our Lord and Savior, we must develop some disciplines in our lives that will help us connect with God:

1. **Bible Reading**—The purpose of reading the Bible is to get to know who God really is and what His character is. When we understand who He is, then we'll better understand how to live a life of faith, which pleases Him (Hebrews 11:6).

2. **Prayer Life**—In any relationship, how do we get to know someone better? By spending time with him or her, asking questions, sharing our thoughts, dreams, and desires. It's the same with God, and that's through prayer—having conversation with God. He instructs us to pray about everything (Philippians 4:6).

3. **Repentance**—The amazing thing to me is that God knows exactly who I am—yet He still loves me (Romans 5:6-8). When we stumble in this walk, it's not cause for us to feel rejection and walk away. Rather, it's an opportunity to confess our sin to the Lord and let Him provide the love and correction we need to get us back on track.

---

*Jon Kitna is quarterback for the Detroit Lions.*

# HEALTH TO THY NAVEL AND MARROW TO THY BONES

JIM WILLIAMS JR. `````````````````````````````````````````````````````

*Be not wise in thine own eyes; fear the Lord, and depart from evil. It shall be health to thy navel, and marrow to thy bones* (Proverbs 3:7-8, KJV).

Earlier this year I was diagnosed with a severe spine infection. After many months of bed rest, massive intravenous antibiotics, and a truckload of pain medications, my health continued to spiral downward. I could not even put on my socks or pick up the paper. My weight was down 20 percent, and I looked like the walking dead.

A team of specialists evaluated my case and recommended immediate surgery requiring a 14-inch incision on my front side to remove my intestines and other vital organs, remove the infection, remove two vertebrae and one disc in my spine and replace them with cadaver bones filled with ground-up bone from my hip. Then they would replace all my organs, sew me up, flip me over, put two rods and many screws into my back for stability, and finally close the incision. Estimated recovery time was 12 to 14 months.

In my weakened condition, I felt that I would die from such surgery. I refer to the day I got this news as Black Thursday. I was released from the hospital for five days to await the surgery and taken off antibiotics in an attempt to get accurate cultures of the organism attacking my spine. During this time a dear friend came to visit me and shared with me Proverbs 3:1-12, which includes the words "Do not be wise in your own eyes; fear the Lord and shun evil. This will bring health to your body and nourishment to your bones" (vv. 7-8). As he read these verses, my spirit leaped within me! God was concerned about the marrow of my bones.

Shortly thereafter, my son sent out an e-mail to a number of Christian elders to request their attendance at a prayer meeting for me. These men met a few days later to pray over me. I was so medicated due to the excruciating pain that I was hardly coherent. Other members of my family fasted and prayed for healing.

My son, who is a physician, started to feel very strongly that the surgery was not the option I should take. After numerous visits and phone calls, he convinced me to postpone the surgery for a few more days. Within those few days I noticed my mobility was increasing and I was requiring fewer pain medications. Day after day, this continued. I had not been taking any medication to fight the infection for over two weeks at this point; however, I was getting better.

Within 10 days of the prayer meeting, I went for a biopsy and two bone scans and was pronounced completely free of all infection. Doctors were astounded at the miraculous healing.

I praise God for his eternal Word and for hiding Proverb 3:7-8 from me until it could save my life! I was too sick to pray for myself, but the Holy Spirit directed me to pray for others in need, and that was the day I started to improve. Prayer works.  📖

---

*Jim Williams Jr. is president of Landplan, Inc. in Frisco, Texas.*

# "WHO DO YOU SAY THAT I AM?"

DAVID BRYANT

From every direction there seems to be increased desire to talk about the Savior. But in his book *Jesus Mean and Wild,* Mike Galli says that we may not be talking about the "real Jesus," stating that "talking about the real Jesus is a dangerous thing." He went on to say that in the New Testament the real Jesus "is a consuming fire, the raging storm, who seems bent on destroying everything in his path, who either shocks people into stupefaction or frightens them so that they run for their lives. . . . He swirls, a tornado touching down, lifting homes and businesses off their foundations, leaving only bits and pieces of the former life strewn on his path. . . . We need to talk with biblical honesty about the One who would not only love and forgive us but also demolish all our cultural images of him." Does this overstate who our Redeemer is?

Remember the debate the Twelve had about Jesus as they walked the roads of Caesarea Philippi? They were responding to Jesus' penetrating question to Peter in Matthew 16: "Who do you say that I am?" Finally Peter answered with the familiar words "You are the Christ, the Son of the living God." But did he or the others really grasp the full implications of that brief sentence? Based on what many scriptures teach about the meaning of those two titles—"the Christ" and "Son of the living God"—Peter's response was equivalent to saying—

- *You are the Superlative One.* You will forever defy all human categories. No language is adequate to describe you. No analysis can fully record all the roles you must play to advance God's ever-expanding kingdom (1 Peter 1).
- *You are the Incomparable One.* You will forever remain in a class by yourself—no duplicates, no clones. Your importance will continue to eclipse all others, outranking every other being in heaven, earth, or hell. You will reign "world without end" (2 Thessalonians 1).
- *You are the Exalted One.* For eternity, you will forever hold the primary focus of our praises, a position of unrivaled distinction, prestige, and majesty in the universe. You will be the joy of all peoples, worthy to receive every treasure, every dominion, and every ounce of praise (Revelation 5).
- *You are the Preeminent One.* In time, in space, in history, and throughout eternity, you will forever lay claim to the universe. As you held the primacy at the beginning, so you will at the end (Colossians 1). All things to come are your possession, to do with as your Father pleases.
- *You are the Sufficient One.* Nothing will ever exhaust your power and resources. You require no "outsourcing." You will forever prove totally adequate for all our longings, fears, needs, or heart cries. You are the final inheritance of each of God's children (Philippians 3).
- *You are the Triumphant One.* None of your enemies will prevail. You will defeat all foes unconditionally—both human

and demonic—to emerge forever unthreatened, unhindered and victorious over all opposition, permanently and forever. You are the everlasting Overcomer (Revelation 17).

- *You are the Unifying One.* Bringing all things under your feet as Lord, you will permanently redeem and reconcile to the God-head innumerable sinners from all the ages and all the nations. In the Consummation, all creation, as well as the Church itself, will be held together in perfect harmony by your irrevocable decrees and your indestructible might (Hebrews 1).

On that red-letter day, Peter was just beginning to wake up to how His Lord was the *focus* of everything the Father deserves, desires, designs, and declares. There in Matthew 16, whether he fully grasped it or not, Peter confessed, "As *Son of God*, wherever you dwell, all God's promises are gathered to you, guaranteed by you, and summed up in you. As *Christ,* you are ordained and anointed as supreme—absolute and universal in every way. You are supreme in the appeal you make to sinners, supreme in the scope of your activities on our behalf, supreme in the depth of your transforming power for all the redeemed, supreme in the irreplaceable ministry of your high priestly work for saints in heaven and earth, supreme in the eternal relevancy of your reign extended throughout the entire universe, supreme in the magnificently indescribable future into which you are taking all who are yours." 📖

---

*David Bryant is CEO of Proclaim Hope! in Providence, New Jersey.*

# THE GREAT PHYSICIAN

GARY SALLQUIST ·················································

*Is any one of you sick? He should call the elders of the church to pray over him and anoint him with oil in the name of the Lord. And the prayer offered in faith will make the sick person well; the Lord will raise him up* (James 5:14-15).

"Great Physician" is one of the many names given to God. One of our family prayers each evening for those in need of healing is—

> *Dear Lord, you are the Great Physician. You alone have the power to heal any and all illnesses and injuries. We know, Lord, that you often choose to use doctors, nurses, medication, counseling, hospitals and therapy to do your healing. There are also times you choose to intervene directly and do it yourself. You are the God of grace, of mercy, of healing, and we ask now for your personal touch for _____. Place your healing hands on him [her], and restore that person to wholeness. Comfort him [her] in the healing process and comfort and strengthen his [her] family. Restore him [her] to full health quickly and completely. In Christ's name we pray. Amen.*

It is true that marvelous medical training, research, and technology often go into the healing of our illnesses and injuries. Behind all that, however, stands the figure of God and His awesome power to heal both directly or indirectly.

When I was at Princeton Theological Seminary years ago, I was privileged to read William Johnson's excellent book *A Physician's Witness to the Power of Shared Prayer.* In this book he shares his own spiritual journey and talks about reaching the point in his life when he could—and would—pray for and with his patients. What a significant impact that had on the healing process of his patients!

As a pastor, I'm keenly aware that sometimes when a person is very ill there are no words—except the names of God, which will bring comfort and peace—to someone who is suffering. But those names will do exactly that, even for a person who doesn't seem to hear but somehow responds. Knowing that God created us, loves us unconditionally, and wants the best for us is deeply and enormously comforting, regardless of how sick or injured we are.

Each and every one of us has already experienced in his or her own life—or the lives of those we love—deep pain and suffering from one cause or another. The Lord never said life would be easy, but He did say that He would be with us every step of the way ("even unto the end of the age") and He is!

When we're feeling good, life is good. When we're hurting, life is tough. Pastor Tim Hansel, who used to have a ministry for inner-city kids, tells this story:

> At the end of some 10 days of adventure, hard work, and being "tested" in the mountains, all the course participants are asked to debrief around the closing campfire. One 10-year-old inner-city kid, when asked what he learned while camping out, hiking, canoeing, rock climbing, and being maxed out by his week-long experience in the mountains of the Great Northwest,

thoughtfully stared into the campfire, stroked his chin, and said, "I learned that life ain't no ride on no pink duck!"

Most of us learn that there are some times when "life ain't no ride on no pink duck!" What a blessing it is to really know that behind the challenges and travails of life, the discomforts and pain of illnesses and injuries, "up there, out there, and back there" is the Creator God who made us, loves us, and heals us! Praise be to God! 📖

---

*Gary Sallquist is headmaster emeritus at Miami Valley Christian Academy in Cincinnati.*

# WHO IS THIS JESUS?

RICK SCHATZ ·················································································

*Jesus replied, "Blessed are you, Simon son of Jonah, for this was not revealed to you by man, but by my Father in heaven"* (Matthew 16:17).

The identity of Jesus is the question of the ages. Many will say He is a good teacher, a prophet, a role model, even a miracle-worker. The disciples saw Jesus' ministry, were witnesses to great miracles, and heard His teachings, including the Sermon on the Mount—yet most of them had doubts about the true identity of Jesus. They questioned whether or not He was the long-awaited Jewish Messiah. They could not comprehend the incarnation with Jesus as the God-man.

Every individual must answer the question about the identity of Christ. When I grew up, I did not have the blessing of a Christian home. We rarely went to church except on Christmas and Easter, yet I never doubted Jesus was the Son of God and that He had died for my sins. But these were only intellectual truths to me and had no impact on my life.

During my second year at the Harvard Business School, my wife, Sharon, encouraged me to join her in going to church. I heard the message of the gospel and believed, not just with my head but also with my heart and soul. My whole life changed when Jesus became the Christ, the Messiah, Lord and King. For the first time in my life, I got off the throne of my own little kingdom and put Jesus on that throne. This change meant that everything in my life was transformed. My goals became to serve God and to bring glory to Him. My words, thoughts, and deeds became captured by the identity of Jesus in my daily living.

Just consider the message we find in Matthew 16 and the impact that the identity of Jesus had on His disciples. These men had followed Christ for three years, and Jesus made them squarely face the question of His identity. Moved by the Holy Spirit, Peter acknowledged that Jesus was the Living God.

As they recognized this truth, the life of every disciple was turned upside down. Their faith grew until they became fully convinced that Jesus was who He said He was. Their faith led them to share the good news of the gospel with an unbelieving world. They spoke with clarity and boldness and were willing to give their lives to share the good news about Jesus as Lord and King.

For every believer and servant of Christ, He is not only Savior but also Lord of everyday living. We're called to live righteously, and as Christian men, we're blessed with the opportunity to be husbands and fathers. We're called to serve our families and to love our wives as Christ loved the Church. Coming to know Jesus as the Christ changes everything. It brings joy, peace, and hope in this life and salvation for the next. ▮▮▮

---

*Rick Schatz is the president and CEO of National Coalition for the Protection of Children & Families.*

# WHAT IS GOD LIKE?

FRANK TUREK ·····················································

*"Who is my equal?" says the Holy One. Lift your eyes and look to the heavens*
(Isaiah 40:25-26).

What is God like? David wrote, "The heavens declare the glory of
God; the skies proclaim the work of his hands" (Psalm 19:1). A couple of centuries later, the prophet Isaiah posed a question from God:
"To whom will you compare me? Or who is my equal?" (40:25). The
answer is in the next verse: "Lift your eyes and look to the heavens.
Who created all these? He who brings out the starry hosts one by
one and calls them each by name. Because of his great power and
mighty strength, not one of them is missing."

How many stars did God create? There are 100 billion stars just
in *our* galaxy, and the average distance between those stars is 30 trillion miles. How far is 30 trillion miles? Let's put it this way: when the
Space Shuttle is in orbit, it travels at about 17,000 miles an hour—
almost 5 miles per second. If you could get in the Space Shuttle and
speed through space at nearly five miles per second, it would take
you 201,450 years to travel 30 trillion miles. In other words, if you

had gotten into the Space Shuttle at the time of Christ and begun traveling from our sun toward another star an average distance away, you would be only one-hundredth of the way there right now!

Now keep in mind that's just between two of the 100 billion stars in *our* galaxy. How many stars are there in the entire universe? A conservative estimate says that the number of stars in the universe is about equal to the number of sand grains on all the beaches of the earth. And at five miles per second, it will take you over 200,000 years to go from one "grain of sand" to another! The heavens are *awesome*.

Why does God tell us to compare Him with the heavens? Because God has no limits, and from our perspective neither do the heavens. God is not a big angel. He is the unlimited limiter, the uncreated Creator of all things. He's the self-existing, infinite Being who created this vast and beautiful universe out of nothing and who holds it all together today. There's only one entity in our experience that can provide an analogy to the infinity of God. Any image intended to depict God just won't do. Any image merely limits his majesty. Only the heavens scream out "infinity."

Infinity is what describes each of God's attributes, including His power, knowledge, justice, and love. This is why the Bible uses the heavens to help us grasp the infinite height of God's love. Psalm 103:11 says, "As high as the heavens are above the earth, so great is his love for those who revere him." That love extends into eternity. So no matter what problem you have, no matter what sin you've committed, no matter how bleak things are, the God of infinite love promises to hold you in His hand forever.  📖

---

*Frank Turek is the president of CrossExamined.org and co-author of* I Don't Have Enough Faith to be an Atheist.

# OUR SIN AGAINST GOD'S CREATION

THEO NICOLAKIS ·····················································

*The heavens declare the glory of God; the skies proclaim the work of his hands* (Psalm 19:1).

One of the most striking sights I have ever experienced was a dramatic sunset from an airplane. In the clouds, fiery reds and brilliant oranges collided with deep hues of purple to form an exploding canvas of colors and movement. The sight was mesmerizing. I sat there transfixed and awestruck as I tried to understand the experience. I finally recalled the words of the Psalmist—"The heavens declare the glory of God; and the firmament shows His handiwork."

As my gaze continued on the unfolding sunset, I saw how fragile the experience was. Slowly, light was overtaken by darkness, and that ever-present human footprint revealed itself in the forms of garbage, pollution, chemical spills, and every other activity that leaves a toxic, human mark on creation. Recognizing humanity as caretakers of God's creation, I was numbed to the core to see the abusive scars we have left.

If we reflect on the current global and ecological crisis, we will readily see that its causes are not only in our gluttonous and overindulgent lifestyles but also because we continue to allow conditions of poverty, the prevalence of social injustice, and the perpetuation of war. These moral conditions both shatter the sacred relationships with each another and also adversely affect God's creation.

How we treat human beings is directly reflected in the way that we relate to the natural environment and to God. By defiling the world God gave us, we also sin against our neighbor, who is impacted by our harmful actions. Harming the environment is an act of sin. It is a result of our transgressions against each other.

We must all repent of our actions and habits that directly or indirectly contaminate God's creation and negatively impact our fellow human beings. From a Christian perspective, being an environmentalist means simultaneously caring for both the environment *and* humanity. One cannot be valued at the expense of the other. We all have a direct responsibility to sanctify creation and offer it back to God.

This perspective has profound implications. Solving our ecological problems ultimately lies with each one of us. While we can achieve nothing without God's help, we cannot simply hand over the environmental problem to God and free ourselves from the responsibility He gave us.

If we truly recognize God as the Creator of all things and heed Jesus' commandment to love our neighbors as ourselves, then we must work harder than ever to be true environmentalists by eradicating conditions of war, restoring social justice, and striving to end world poverty. Only then can we preserve the majesty of God's creation so that future generations will be able to partake of the world that declares the glory of God. ▮▮▮

*Theo Nicolakis is director of information technology for the Greek Orthodox Archdiocese of America.*

# BUILDING YOUR HOUSE
# UPON THE ROCK

DAVE BROWN ·····························································

Recently I was in northern California for a family wedding. I had never been to Santa Cruz before and was able to enjoy my daily exercise in some delightful walks by the beach. In the midst of much beauty, I was awestruck watching the waves crashing against the rocks. It was impressive to see the irresistible force of the ocean meet the unmovable object of the craggy cliff. The water sprayed against the rock. The rock withstood the crashing tide. The ocean's inexorable force pounded again and again, but the jagged precipice remained solid and sure.

As I watched nature play out this action, I thought of life. It seems that many times we get pounded by the crashing surf of life. Do we build our lives upon that which is firm and strong and stands against the storms of life? We know that the Word of God is a rock, unchanging amid the shifting sands and the tribulations of life. Indeed, Jesus said, "In the world ye shall have tribulation: but be of good cheer; I have overcome the world" (John 16:33, KJV). And yet so often we look for strength not from God or His Word but in ourselves. How sad! How unwise! Like the disciples of old, we, too, are "slow of heart" to learn.

Jesus said,

> Everyone who hears these words of mine and puts them into practice is like a wise man who built his house on the rock. The rain came down, the streams rose, and the winds blew and beat against that house; yet it did not fall, because it had its foundation on the rock. But everyone who hears these words of mine and does not put them into practice is like a foolish man who built his house on sand. The rain came down, the streams rose, and the winds blew and beat against that house, and it fell with a great crash (*Matthew 7:24-27*).

What is it that you put your trust in for security against the storms of life? Could it be your job, your family, your accomplishments in community, or church? How about key relationships that are dear to you? Could it even be your imperfect but faithful service to the Lord?

Storms will come into the life of every believer; indeed, they seem to come with great ferocity into the lives of some of God's choicest servants. So where do we turn? How do we build? Hopefully not with "wood, hay, stubble" (1 Corinthians 3:12, KJV) but with precious stones. The foundation cornerstone is clearly salvation by grace through faith in our Lord Jesus. We then grow in the Lord by that same merciful grace, applying the Word of God, fellowship and worship with others, prayer, the ordinances that the Lord provides as means of grace (baptism and the Lord's Supper/Communion), and reaching out with the gospel to those who don't yet know Christ. I'm reminded of the words of Martin Luther's great hymn based on Psalm 46: "A mighty fortress is our God, / a Bulwark never failing; / Our Helper He, amid the flood / Of mortal ills prevailing."

No doubt our journey is fraught with "many dangers, toils, and snares" but we remind ourselves that "'tis grace that's brought us safe thus far, and grace will lead us home." And surely we can agree that the preeminent grace was when God in His kindness wooed and won our hearts to faith in His Son, "In whom we have redemption through the forgiveness of sins" (Ephesians 1:7, KJV).

But again, we must "grow in grace and the knowledge of the truth" (2 Peter 3:18), not remaining children in the faith but being doers of the Word of Jesus and not merely hearers who deceive ourselves (James 2:22-24). From beginning to end, we come to God by grace through faith to worship Him for who He is and for what He's done—and to heed the words of our Savior Christ Jesus, who calls all people everywhere to repent and believe in Him, and live changed lives by His grace, which enables our lifelong obedience and trust in His holy Word.

A big part of surviving the storms of life is that we turn back again and again to God and His Word. While it is no doubt good and even crucial to engage our culture in dialogue and deed, we all need a more sure word, namely the Word of God working in our hearts and lives by the Holy Spirit. Then we must hear and obey the words of Jesus. Rightly did the apostle Peter say, "The grass withers and the flowers fall, but the word of the Lord stands forever. And this is the word that was preached to you" (1 Peter 1:24-25).

To Him alone be the glory!  ▮▮▮

---

*Dave Brown is director of counseling and support for National Coalition for the Protection of Children & Families.*

# FREE INDEED

MIKE PLATTER ·····················································

*"If you abide in My word, you are My disciples indeed. And you shall know the truth, and the truth shall make you free." They answered Him, "We are Abraham's descendants, and have never been in bondage to anyone. How can You say, 'You will be made free'?" Jesus answered them, "Most assuredly, I say to you, whoever commits sin is a slave of sin. And a slave does not abide in the house forever, but a son abides forever. Therefore if the Son makes you free, you shall be free indeed"* (John 8:31-36, NKJV).

About 100 miles from Athens, overlooking the Pleistos River, is the site of the ancient city of Delphi. For hundreds of years, before and after the birth of Christ, Delphi was considered by the pagans to be blessed by the gods. In particular, the famed "Oracle of Delphi" could be sought out for her knowledge of the future, and her answers were given for a price.

While on a tourist visit there, I saw something quite surprising. It was a stone wall on which were etched more than a thousand names, all from before the year 100 A.D. The guide explained that these were the names of slaves who were being set free by their masters. The technical term was "manumission," and there were specific conditions required for the release of these slaves. One of those conditions was that a price had to be paid to the gods and that the authority of that god then mediated the slave's freedom. The money was given at Delphi, and the slave's name was entered upon the wall as proof that there would be freedom in his or her future.

I stared for quite a while at those names carved in Greek letters onto the stones. It occurred to me that perhaps some of those former slaves later visited Delphi with their families. I envisioned them pointing to their own name on the wall and proudly saying, "This was the day my new life began—this was the day that our family had a chance to be free."

I was struck by the parallels with those of us who have come to know Christ. We were once slaves—unable to be free from the bondage of sin in our lives. We could not free ourselves—a price had to be paid for us. And, of course, it was God who paid for our freedom through the sacrificial life, death and resurrection of Jesus, His own Son.

We need to be reminded from time to time that there is a lifestyle that belongs to those who are free, just as there are behaviors that belong to those who are still slaves. The Bible tells us that sin made us slaves but that Christ has made us free. We must remember that certain behaviors can enslave us and take away the very freedom that Christ has given us. Those things we call sin can bind us just as surely as any iron chains. So we pray and ask God for the strength, honesty, and commitment to live as free men, to stay far away from the chains that used to bind us when we were slaves to sin. 📖

*Mike Platter is senior pastor of Glendora Community Church of the Nazarene.*

# FINDING MY WAY

**PAUL RADER** ·······················································

The advent of GPS (global positioning system) technology was a godsend for me, partly because I'm directionally challenged but mostly because I just like to know where I'm going and how long it might take to get there. Having direction from satellites has lowered my blood pressure considerably, although I have learned that even with the best of these devices, I must pay attention and use some common sense. The best part of it is that when, even with the help of my GPS, I manage to get lost anyway, eventually it can get me back on track.

All my life I have been trying to find my way. Life for me, and maybe for you, has been an adventure in search and discovery. Not that direction has been unavailable. We have God's promise: "I will instruct you and teach you in the way you should go; I will counsel you and watch over you" (Psalm 32:8). That does not ensure turn-by-turn directions in every instance. Sometimes the instructions may be clear: "This is the way; walk in it" (Isaiah 30:21). "Do not set foot on the path of the wicked or walk in the way of evil men" (Proverbs 4:14).

In fact, if we're listening with an open heart, we have far more clear guidance available to us than we tend to access. And this I know: to turn aside from what I clearly understand to be God's desire for me leads to darkness, confusion, and pain. It would be bad enough if it involved only me. Life being what it is, inevitably others are affected by the wrong turns I might take.

Often enough, God leaves me in no doubt as to the way I should take. Even so, as a general rule I find that we are pointed in the right general direction by the instruction we gain from God's Word. The goal is made clear, and then we're expected to find our own way. God intends for us to internalize the teaching of His Word and then sensitize ourselves to the nudging of His Spirit through the discipline of prayer. Beyond that, He does us the honor of expecting us to pay attention and use our sanctified common sense in sorting out the options with which life presents us.

In all of this we have the security of knowing that His loving eye is upon us. "He guards the course of the just and protects the way of his faithful ones" (Proverbs 2:8). Even when our stubbornness and self-will get us off track, if we're prepared to admit our predicament and our failure to find our way, He will show us a way back into the path of his purpose for us. It may not be Plan A. But in the end, it will get us home.

Best of all, Jesus himself, the Way, shares the journey with us. ▮▮

---

*Paul A. Rader is a retired general in the Salvation Army.*

# THE SOBERING SIDE OF SUCCESS

BOB RECCORD ·················································

*After Uzziah became powerful, his pride led to his downfall* (2 Chronicles 26:16).

In his in-your-face book *The Success Fantasy,* Tony Compolo says of success, "As children we dream of it; we strive for it through our adult lives, and we suffer melancholy in old age if we have not reached it."

Success is so often sought only to find that it's not nearly what we thought it would be when it comes. It seems to carry with it the law of diminishing returns—the more of it we get, the less we are satisfied, and the more we think we need. It simply reveals that the key problem at the core of our being is that there is a God-shaped hole in all of us that nothing can fill—not a person, a position, a promotion, or a possession. Only God can manage that.

So it was with one of the most successful men in the Old Testament—King Uzziah. He was so successful in his time that the writer Isaiah marked one of the most significant events in his own life by the death of Uzziah.

Read his story in 2 Chronicles 26, and you'll be amazed that he was launched into his success at the wise old age of 16, and then led his nation for 52 years. The Bible touts his resumé. There's enough there to cover three lifetimes, let alone one! He was a leader, civil engineer, developer, strategist, military leader, city planner, and head of his entire nation. Not bad, don't you agree?

And he accomplished it all through God's help. But then came the sobering side of success—pride. And that led to his downfall. Overly self-confident, taking credit rather than giving the credit to God, unfaithful to the One who had been so faithful to him, convinced he was beyond failure—what a recipe for failure! And we all stare it in the face at different times of our own journeys.

Pride will inevitably lead to a downfall. Pride makes everything about ourselves—what *we* have accomplished, what *we* want, what *we* need. The Hebrew term for pride carries the idea of "lifting up and being haughty." And that's indeed what we do—lift up ourselves and become haughty for what we take credit for. And that blinds us to the danger of stupid steps. For Uzziah it led to stepping into an arena that God had told him was not his to enter. And he refused to be accountable to those who tried to warn him.

Sound familiar? I notice it in today's language when I hear men say things like "I can handle it," "This once won't matter," and "I don't mean for anyone to get hurt." But the sad fact is we *can't* handle it, once *does* matter, and someone *always* gets hurt.

So be careful of what you hope for. Success has its merits, but it also has its sobering side. Remember: we're all only one step from stupid at any given moment!  ▥

---

*Bob Reccord is the president and CEO of Total Life Impact Ministries.s*

# ACCOUNTABILITY

GARY SALLQUIST ·······························································

*Each of us will give an account of himself to God* (Romans 14:12).

In Rod Handley's exceptional *Character Counts* ministry, the question is "Character counts—who's counting yours?" None of us are called to be Lone Ranger Christians. Time and again throughout Scripture, God calls us to be Christians in community, to serve each other and to serve *with* each other. An integral part of the serving process is integrity. An integral part is earning trust. An integral part is accountability. That's often a man's least favorite ingredient.

One of the active topics in both the workplace and in the life of the Church is mentoring. One aspect of being mentored is being accountable. That entails an environment, a process, and committed brothers in the Lord.

Rod Handley's book includes a list of questions for accountability group partners, the last of which is "For which of the above questions, in your answers you gave us today, did you lie to us?" That's going right to the heart of the matter. Sometimes we lie to ourselves.

A question like that prevents us from skating by when dealing with life's important issues regarding our Christian walk and lifestyle.

Over the years it has been my privilege to be a part of seven different accountability groups. Those groups have met at varying times at various locations ranging from coffee shops to fast food restaurants to theological seminaries.

The sites themselves are not important as long as there is relative privacy, an endless supply of hot coffee, a commitment by everybody to be there on time—and every time they're in town—and usually at least snacks, depending on the time of the meeting. Twenty-four of us have been accountability partners together over the years. Some of us have been in several groups together.

When I had the privilege of serving on Promise Keepers' national staff, I remember reading a survey that pointed out the single greatest problem for the American man is loneliness—the John Wayne mentality of trying to do life in isolation. It's true, as John Donne said so long ago, "No man is an island." No man is—or at least he shouldn't be—an island.

However busy you are, wherever your schedule takes you, you'll do yourself a great favor by meeting regularly (preferably weekly) with a group of Christian brothers who will share with you, mentor you, love you, challenge you, support you, and change you like my 24 accountability group partners have done for me. We are indeed, as Romans 14:12 says, accountable to God. We are accountable to God *through* and *to* each other. In this life of Christian living, we're indeed all in this together. ▐▌

---

*Gary Sallquist is headmaster emeritus at Miami Valley Christian Academy in Cincinnati.*

# YOU CANNOT MANAGE SIN

CHUCK STECKER ··················································

*Later Jesus found him at the temple and said to him, "See, you are well again. Stop sinning or something worse may happen to you"* (John 5:14).

The phone call is as clear today as it was a few years ago. It was a regular phone check-up with a very close friend to see how he was doing. He had been battling alcoholism for years and had been in and out of different rehab programs.

I asked him how he was doing with the alcohol issue, and he responded with the almost-normal reply "Not bad. I seem to be doing better." Then it hit me—he was okay with his drinking. He just wanted to get it to an acceptable level. He wanted to get his life right but still be able to drink.

It was one of those incredible wake-up calls for me. My friend was like most men. We think that we can beat the problem by working our way out of it. You know—gradually getting to where we want to be in life.

We think that we can establish acceptable levels of sin that will in some way be pleasing to God.

In doing so, it allows us to continue to sin, only to what we perceive as a lesser degree so we can report that we're "doing better."

So often we like to compare ourselves and our lives with really bad sins so our lives, by comparison, don't look that bad. It's as if we're saying, "Come on—give me a break. I didn't kill anyone today."

We want to ignore the sin as we let our eyes wander and even dwell on ladies inappropriately. We say to ourselves, a little look won't hurt; after all, I'm getting better.

We spew out a few curse words but justify them by the heat of the moment; but again, we're "getting better." Isn't that what God wants? Jesus did not tell the man, "Go and sin less each day, and eventually you'll become healed and free from this thing." He said, "Go and sin no more."

Sin is sin. God does not give us acceptable levels that are more pleasing to Him than others. There are not degrees of sin that are established by comparison with others to make us feel that we're "doing better."

One of the most important steps is to look at our lives and genuinely ask the question "Where have I established acceptable levels of sin in my life?"

Perhaps it's time to really listen to Jesus when He said, "Stop sinning." Pray and ask God to show you where you have established "acceptable levels" of sin, and ask Him to give you the strength to stop sinning. Start with one area of your life, and refuse to believe Satan when He says that some sin will be okay today. As a result, your progress will then be pleasing to God. 📖

---

*Chuck Stecker is founder and president of A Chosen Generation, Littleton, Colorado.*

# FOUR IMPORTANT LESSONS

MIKE CAMBRON ·····················································

*Resist the devil, and he will flee from you (James 4:7).*
*Not by might, nor by power, but by my spirit, saith the Lord of hosts (Zechariah 4:6, KJV).*

I learned four important lessons on a recent overseas trip. In late August I flew 24 hours returning from South Africa; a day later I traveled to Washington, D.C., for two extended meetings. My internal clock was totally out of whack. I awoke at 1:30 A.M. in my hotel room and fought to go back to sleep. At 8:00 A.M. I was scheduled for a four-hour meeting where I would be the featured presenter. I determined to go back to sleep with little luck; my mind meandered through random prayers, agenda items, thoughts of politics, and vain imaginations. At 2:30 A.M. I was still restless. Finally, I got up to read a book.

Sometimes life crashes in on us. *The battle belongs to the Lord,* I told myself. *Live not by the flesh, but by the spirit of God. My strength is in the Lord.* I looked in the hotel nightstand for a Gideon's Bible, but I didn't find one. I had other spiritual armor with me, though; Watchman Nee's *The Release of the Spirit* and Oswald Chambers' *My Utmost for His Highest.* I spent two hours with these heroes of the faith and was refreshed, energized, and victorious. During that long night I learned some truths I hope I'll never forget.

**Lesson 1:** Resisting in the flesh always fails. Christians are built to run on God and God alone. Victory does not come through our own virtues—strength, character, knowledge. or experience. It is not what *we bring* but what God puts in us.

**Lesson 2:** Alcohol or any other escape mechanism would only have complicated my life and inhibited my ability to respond to the call of God.

**Lesson 3:** When prayers seem to go unanswered, God is trying to tell you something. Search for it. For me that night, it was that resisting in my flesh leads to compromise and failure. I need to ask God for eyes to see what He wants to do in me.

**Lesson 4:** When we escape temptation, we must bow our heads and worship. For it is by His grace alone!

O Holy Spirit, breathe afresh on me! (1 Cor 1:26-30; Gal 2:20). 📖

---

*Mike Cambron is a senior executive with Barlett & Company, Cincinnati, Ohio.*

# STOP

J. K. WARRICK ·····································

*Since we have a great high priest who has gone through the heavens, Jesus the Son of God, let us hold firmly to the faith we profess. For we do not have a high priest who is unable to sympathize with our weaknesses, but we have one who has been tempted in every way, just as we are—yet was without sin. Let us then approach the throne of grace with confidence, so that we may receive mercy and find grace to help us in our time of need* (Hebrews 4:14-16).

"Let *us* hold firmly." We are responsible to get a good grip on our faith, even in the face of temptation. Jesus has faced every temptation known to us—*a high priest who has been tempted in every way, just as we are*—and He promises that as we come before Him, we will discover mercy (thank God for His mercy!) and grace to help in our times of need.

Grace is not an excuse for bad behavior; grace is help in the time of need, and in the scripture for today the need is for strength to face temptation. I recently heard a pastor say he was "learning to live at the foot of the Cross in the power of the Resurrection"—living at the foot of the Cross (the place of mercy) in the power of the Resurrection (grace to help in the time of need).

How can we do that when we're all alone and facing powerful temptation? Let me give you a handy tool to work with, using the acronym STOP.

**S**—"Since, then, you have been raised with Christ, set your hearts on things above, where Christ is seated at the right hand of God" (Colossians 3:1).

**T**—"Trust in the Lord with all your heart and lean not on your own understanding; in all your ways acknowledge him, and he will make your paths straight" (Proverbs 3:5-6).

**O**—"Offer yourselves to God, as those who have been brought from death to life; and offer the parts of your body to him as instruments of righteousness" (Romans 6:13).

**P**—"Press on toward the goal to win the prize for which God has called me heavenward in Christ Jesus" (Philippians 3:14).

Every time you pull up to a stop sign, remember these scriptures, and rely on the promise of our Lord to come alongside in your time of temptation.

No temptation has seized you except what is common to man. And God is faithful; he will not let you be tempted beyond what you can bear. But when you are tempted, he will also provide a way out so that you can stand up under it (*1 Corinthians 10:13*).

*Prayer: God and Father of our Lord Jesus Christ, extend mercy to us in our weakness and grace to make us strong. In Jesus' name we pray. Amen.* 📖

---

*J. K. Warrick is general superintendent of the International Church of the Nazarene.*

# APPENDIX 1
## NATIONAL COALITION FOR THE PROTECTION OF CHILDREN AND FAMILIES

Human sexuality is a gift from God, meant to be celebrated. However, this gift has been distorted, producing pain, guilt, shame, and brokenness.

National Coalition for the Protection of Children and Families has been called to lead the charge to restore biblical sexuality in America. Since its founding in 1983, National Coalition has accomplished a great deal in its mission *to move the people of God to embrace, live out, preserve, and advance the truth of biblical sexuality.*

Over the years, Coalition leaders have met with two presidents and five attorneys general. In addition, it has influenced the policies of some of the nation's largest corporations, including Abercrombie & Fitch, General Motors, AT&T, and leading wireless companies.

But more importantly, it has impacted the lives of countless individuals, marriages, and children. Through its headquarters in Cincinnati and seven regional offices in Atlanta, Charlotte, Columbus, Kansas City, New England, Seattle, and St. Louis, the Coalition has built partnerships with hundreds of churches, Christian schools, seminaries, and para-church ministries.

We thank God for what has been accomplished through National Coalition thus far. With the help of fervent warriors, and the guidance and power of Almighty God, this ministry will continue to serve the nation through its three key strategies:

- Protecting the Vulnerable
- Restoring the Broken
- Engaging the Culture

It is the hope and prayer of our members that this devotional book will provide a healthy, godly alternative for men who travel. Rather than accessing adult pay-per-view channels in hotel rooms, we pray men will turn to these uplifting, challenging, and encouraging devotionals.

In addition to this devotional book, National Coalition offers the following resources to help those struggling with pornography, sexual addiction, and the sexualized messages of the culture:

- Confidential HelpLine (800-583-2964)
- For Men Only support and accountability groups
- Cultural Apologetics Series
- PowerPoint presentations
- *What Every Parent Needs to Know About* booklet series

For more information on resources, please visit www.national-coalition.org.

# CHURCH OF THE NAZARENE

The Church of the Nazarene is the largest Protestant Christian church in the classical Wesleyan-Holiness tradition, tracing its roots to an anniversary date of 1908. It was founded to spread the message of scriptural holiness (Christlike living) around the world.

The Church of the Nazarene is a Great Commission church. Nazarenes are passionate about making a difference in the world by taking the good news of Jesus Christ to people everywhere. We believe that God offers forgiveness, peace, joy, purpose, love, meaning in life, and the promise of heaven when life is over to everyone who enters into a personal relationship with Him through Jesus Christ. We are called to take this message to the world.

Today, the Church of the Nazarene ministers in 151 world areas, and approximately 800 Nazarene missionaries and volunteers serve in those locations. Nazarenes worship in more than 212 languages or tribal languages, with literature produced in 90 of these. The church operates 64 medical clinics and hospitals worldwide. This missionary enterprise is made possible by the contributions of the global Nazarene family. Nazarenes are also engaged in starting new churches and congregations by praying, giving, and supporting worldwide volunteers and contracted missionaries.

The Church of the Nazarene views human sexuality as one expression of the holiness and beauty that God the Creator intended for His creation. It is one of the ways by which the covenant between a husband and a wife is sealed and expressed. Sexuality misses its purpose when treated as an end in itself or when cheapened by pornographic and perverted sexual interests.

It is the hope and prayer of the Adult Ministries International staff of the Church of the Nazarene that this devotional book will challenge men to focus upon God and His purposes. There is no limit to what God can do through men who put God's plans and purposes above that of their own desires.

In additional to the devotional book, Adult Ministries has many other resources to help men grow spiritually and find fulfillment in Christ. Information about these resources is made available through the following Web sites and personnel.

**Contact Information**
Wm Marshall Duke, International Men's Ministries Coordinator
Larry R. Morris, Director of Adult Ministries International
17001 Prairie Star Parkway
Lenexa Kansas 66220
Toll-free: 1.877.240.2417
E-mail: adultministries@nazarene.org
or
mensministries@nazarene.org
Web sites:
adultministries.nazarene.org
amc.nazarene.org
clt.nazarene.org

# APPENDIX 2

## LIVING A LIFE OF SEXUAL PURITY IN A XXX CULTURE

RICK SCHATZ

**The Challenge**

We live in a hyper-sexualized culture, and all of us are challenged by the messages of the world. As we live in this culture, our concerns must be our personal integrity and purity, our marriages, and our children. The battle for purity is not just about behavior but also includes our thoughts and our worldviews, which are expressions of how we think about our relationship to Christ and how we follow Him as Lord and Savior.

We must understand some of the lies of our sexualized culture and how they impact us. These lies include—

- Sex any time, any way, under any circumstances with anyone is not only okay but beneficial as well.
- Marriage is boring and irrelevant.
- Cohabitation is better than marriage.
- No one is faithful in marriage.
- No young person is able to lead a life of sexual purity.
- Pornography is a victimless crime, and no one is harmed by its use.

The sources of these sexualized messages include television, movies, music, advertising, magazines, and the Internet. This content is also available through video cell phones, iPods, PDAs and portable PlayStations.

### The Results

The bottom line is that we as Christian men, including pastors and faith leaders, are not doing well in facing the challenges of our sexualized culture.

- Pornography and sexually oriented businesses gross more revenue that major league baseball, NBA basketball, and NFL football combined—more than $15 billion per year in the United States alone.
- Premarital sex among our teens and young adults is rampant.
- The American teenager is the most sexually active teenager in the industrialized world.
- Cohabitation is now viewed as an acceptable and even honorable alternative to marriage.
- The divorce rate among Christians is higher than that outside the Church.
- Christian men are struggling, with over 60 percent of those who attend Promise Keepers conferences indicating that sexual purity is the number-one issue they face in their walk with Christ.

### The Goal

Living for Christ in our sexualized culture means not just abstaining from immoral sexual activity but also living a life of genuine purity of mind, heart, word, and deed. Our goal must be purity, intimacy with God, and intimacy with others.

We must understand that sex is God's wonderful gift to men and women (Genesis 1:26-27), but its use is to be confined to covenantal heterosexual marriage between one man and one woman. This gift of sexuality is to be celebrated within marriage (Genesis 2:24), recognizing that all other sexual relationships are violations of His will and are harmful (Galatians 6:7-10).

God's gift of sexuality is a blessing (Jeremiah 29:11; John 10:10). His concern is not just our behavior but our thought lives as well (Matthew 5:27-30; Job 31:1). God desires that we have strong marriages, families with children, and young adults who are living lives of sexual purity.

One of our problems in living in our sexualized world is that we do not understand that God's calling is one of holiness, not happiness. We are called to obedience (John 14:21) and to press toward the goal of righteousness in Christ (Philippians 3:12-14).

### The Problem

Few men start out, in terms of sexual failure, by using hardcore pornography or engaging in affairs. Rather, it's much more likely that our initial struggle is seen in more subtle behavior. This is often seen in telling jokes or participating in inappropriate sexual discussion, channel surfing in attempts to see sexual content, wandering eyes, flirting with members of the opposite sex, and unwillingness to discuss sexual intimacy with our spouses.

Sometimes these initial indications of a problem move to the level of an addiction. This is likely the case for 15 percent to 20 percent of the Christian men in our nation—some would say even higher. The sexual addict is an individual who wants to stop certain behaviors and thought patterns but is simply unable to do so.

### Strategy for Victory

Living a life of purity, one that honors Christ in our sexualized culture, is a daunting but not impossible task. Our first step is to make a personal commitment to living a life of purity. This must include recognition of the blessing of righteousness and the power and harm of sin. Our goal must be to live with Christ as Lord in every element of our lives, including our sexual behavior and thought lives.

Victory will escape us if we try to win this battle by ourselves. God has made us for fellowship, and we must stand together in this battle (Proverbs 27:17). We must love our wives as Christ loved the Church (Ephesians 5:25) and allow our wives to hold us accountable as we guard our eyes and live for Christ. Winning the day also means we must raise our children to follow the Lord and to lead lives of purity themselves. Where appropriate, we must face the reality of sexual addiction and take steps to overcome the problem before it destroys us, our marriages, and our families.

A strategy for victory recognizes that this is a spiritual war. We must pray continually for God's strength (1 Thessalonians 5:15-17), put on the whole armor or God (Ephesians 6:10-18), confess and repent of any sexual sin (James 5:15), and make sure we're in right relationship with our wives (1 Peter 3:7).

Winning the day for our children requires us to be informed about the realities of the sexualized culture in which they're living, the sexualized messages they're receiving, and the challenges they face. Ignorance is not bliss. We must recognize that sex education is taking place with our children all the time; the only question is the source. Thus, we must talk to our kids about sex regularly and consistently no matter how challenging or difficult it is.

We must face the reality that the sexualized messages of the culture can destroy our marriages. The threat to our marriages does not simply mean refraining from sexual intercourse with others, but it includes a breakdown of intimacy, which is emotional, spiritual, and physical. We must recognize that building strong, lasting marriages takes work and commitment.

The great news is that no sexual sin is unpardonable sin; it is all covered by the cross of Christ. As we confess, repent, and live for Jesus, we're cleansed from all unrighteousness. The Holy Spirit lives in the heart of each believer and gives to the person who is totally sold out to Christ the power to live a holy life. This is our calling, our challenge, and our blessing. 📖

# NOTES

## Foreword

1. "Characteristics of U. S. Business Owners," 2002 Economic Census, September 2006, U. S. Department of Commerce, Economics and Statistics Administration, and the U. S. Census Bureau.

2. "America on the Go," Findings from the National Household Travel Survey, October 2003, U. S. Department of Transportation, Bureau of Transportation Statistics.

3. "About The Hotel Networks," <www.thehotelnetworks.com>.

4. Nielsen Report, September 2008.

5. Alternative lodging is available at <www.CleanHotels.com>. Here access is provided to a network of lodging facilities that do not offer in-room, "adult," pay-per-view movies. At the web site, simply click on "Find a Hotel," and then enter the city to which you're traveling; you'll then have access to a list of hotels in that city where pay-per-view is *not* offered. You'll see the price range for a nightly rate, a "star" rating, a brief description, and then a list of amenities for that hotel. Your booking not only helps to protect yourself, but it also supports a facility that cares enough about the well-being of its customers not to make harmful programming available.

6. "About Us," statistics as of November 2008, <www.lodgenet.com>.

7. *Promo Magazine,* as quoted in "Overview," <www.thehotelnetworks.com>.

8. Ibid.